"Almost everything I've learned about pedagogy I've learned from David Smith. This book is another gem from a master teacher of teachers. Attuned to the gritty particularity of classroom experiences, Smith invites teachers into habits of reflection about what they do every day, so that they may become increasingly attentive to how faith is carried in concrete practices. In this book, you will recognize the most mundane moments of your teaching day but see them in a new light—filled with possibility for faith formation."

—**James K. A. Smith**
professor of philosophy, Calvin University

"David I. Smith's *Everyday Christian Teaching* is a welcome transformative resource for all educators. As a prominent voice in Christian education across the globe, Smith challenges educators to examine how their practices reflect their convictions as followers of Christ. Through engaging narratives and examples, Smith offers a journey for the reader that not only inspires but also equips through practical prompts. It is an invitation for educators to reflect—then act—on how the biblical story must shape teaching and learning. It is an invitation to consider deeply our 'everyday' being. *Everyday Christian Teaching* is an essential addition to any educator's library, and a must read for all involved in Christian teacher formation."

—**Fiona Partridge**
principal, National Institute for Christian Education, Australia

"There is something both 'everyday' and 'once in a lifetime' about this tremendous invitation from David Smith to look for wisdom in all of your pedagogical habits and learning encounters. Whether you are a young or well-seasoned educator, walk with Smith and reflect intentionally on the way of wisdom in your classroom; you won't regret taking those first steps."

—**Beth Green**
provost and chief academic officer, Tyndale University, Canada

"*Everyday Christian Teaching* meets the desperate need to help Christians teach faithfully in pluralistic institutions by offering thoughtful, winsome, and practical reflections rooted deeply in the Christian tradition."

—**Daniel G. Hummel**
director of the Lumen Center, Madison, Wisconsin

"David Smith's *On Christian Teaching* called us to examine the intersections between our faith commitments and our teaching practices. Now, in *Everyday Christian Teaching*, Smith invites us to look more deeply at our classroom liturgies—the rhythms, exchanges, pauses, and engagements that shape the daily dance of teaching and learning. Through compelling narrative, real-life examples, and practical exercises, this worthy sequel activates our imagination around what is possible in our own practice. When it comes to connecting our faith and teaching more fully, Smith uses the metaphor of pilgrimage; it is the wise teacher who counts Smith as a guide for the journey."

—**Lynn Swaner**
president, Cardus US

"Practical, provocative, and profound, this wise book invites readers to attend to what it looks like to hold faith and teaching together. It has already shaped the way I teach."

—**Ted A. Smith**
director of the Theological Education between the Times project and author of *The End of Theological Education*

"Through reflective storytelling from his extensive experience, David Smith offers his readers profound insights into how Christian faith can be powerfully communicated through everyday teaching practices and habitual teacher behaviors. Every Christian teacher needs to read this book."

—**Trevor Cooling**
emeritus professor of Christian education, Canterbury Christ Church University, UK

"David Smith is America's foremost authority on thinking Christianly about pedagogy. In characteristically clear and engaging prose, *Everyday Christian Teaching* extends Smith's analysis to particular actions and tactical decisions that make up the daily craft of the Christian teacher. The book is essential reading for anyone seeking to live and work faithfully as a Christian educator."

—**Rick Ostrander**
executive director of the Michigan Christian Study Center, Ann Arbor, Michigan

EVERYDAY CHRISTIAN TEACHING

A Guide to Practicing Faith in the Classroom

David I. Smith

William B. Eerdmans Publishing Company
Grand Rapids, Michigan

Wm. B. Eerdmans Publishing Co.
2006 44th Street SE, Grand Rapids, MI 49508
www.eerdmans.com

Published 2025

Book design by Lydia Hall

Printed in the United States of America

31 30 29 28 27 26 25 3 4 5 6 7

ISBN 978-0-8028-8300-1

Library of Congress Cataloging-in-Publication Data

A catalog record for this book is available from the Library of Congress.

CONTENTS

INVITATION

ORBIS PICTUS: INVITATION

INVITATION TO WISDOM

"Come, child! Learn to be wise."

This book is about teaching, so let's begin by imagining ourselves as learners. Imagine yourself a student in a schoolroom somewhere in Germany in the late seventeenth century. You are settling down for the start of a Latin class. There is a new textbook, lavishly illustrated with images, each of which is accompanied by a short narrative. What first greets you is a chapter headed "Invitation," with an image of a teacher and a child standing by a road.[1]

This probably doesn't strike you as particularly odd. You have not learned Latin in other schools, in other times and places, just this one. You have not compared all the different ways of starting a textbook. As far as you know, this beginning is just the way things are in language classrooms. Perhaps it has to be this way. Perhaps Latin classes have always begun like this.

As you look closer, you notice that the child in the picture has taken off his hat and is inclining his ear to listen. Apparently, this is a well-raised child. He has learned some manners and is ready to enter school. Behind him are dark, clouded skies and a thicket of trees and bushes. One tree branch at his elbow touches the ground, a symbolic hint of mortality. But the child is facing away from the tangle and shadow, away from the sin and ignorance of unformed human nature. He is taking some initial steps along a road that leads into sunlight and community. Standing by the road with him is a pilgrim guide. Perhaps you could travel along with them. The first words beneath the picture, in Latin and your mother tongue, are:

"Come, child! Learn to be wise."

Now imagine yourself a teacher in the same schoolroom. You are starting Latin class with a new textbook. You open it at the first chapter, and you are in the picture, too; there is a teacher standing by a road next to a child. He points to rays of light that stream over his shoulder toward the student's upturned face. You have prepared at least a few pages ahead, so you know that these rays will soon appear again in another image, this time representing the glory of God. This teacher is not the source of the truth that gives authority to his teaching, nor is the presence that makes his teaching fruitful ultimately his own. He is cooperating with a grace that is greater than his grasp. Oddly, he is not standing in a schoolroom, or even in a town. He is out amid the dangers of the open road, dressed as a pilgrim. The road that the student must travel is one that the teacher walks as well, both traveling together toward wisdom. The text beneath the image reads:

> Teacher: Come, child! Learn to be wise.
> Child: What is that, to be wise?
> Teacher: To understand rightly, act rightly, and speak rightly all that is necessary.
> Child: Who will teach me this?
> Teacher: I, with God.

You take a closer look at the road. As it runs from left to right, from dim entanglement to the grace of day, it takes a sharp left turn. It runs up between the staff and the cloak of the teacher, between the staff of moral authority and the cloak of academic authority, under the shining rays of divine authority. The path of learning involves moral, intellectual, and spiritual formation.[2] It is a narrow path that will lead to knowledge, but also to faith and character, sustained by grace and hope. It leads to the entrance to a town, where learner and teacher are to take up their places as responsible, mature contributors to a just and flourishing community. This pilgrim road is not just about getting from A to B but about who we will be when we arrive.

This is the first day of class. What has to happen the next day, and the day after, if this opening vision is to be more than a flash of deceptive advertising? What kind of learning practices might make this an everyday pilgrimage and not just a noble burst of enthusiasm? What kind of teacher could offer such an invitation and hope to be taken seriously, and how might one become that kind of teacher?

"Come, child! Learn to be wise."

WALKING THE ROAD

This book is about learning to teach wisely. One of the moments that provoked it occurred a few years ago during an online presentation to faculty at a Christian university. Our focus was on how our teaching practices can draw from Christian faith and contribute to students' spiritual growth. I avoided offering a high-altitude pep talk about how faith ought to shape our teaching. I spent the bulk of the time focusing on the concrete, illustrating through examples how beliefs and values can shape decisions about learning. I hoped I was being quite practical.

One participant's question at the end of the presentation stuck with me. "I have taught at this Christian university for several years," he said. "I believe in its mission. I have also been actively involved in a local church over the same time span. I worship there regularly. But I would never have made the connections between the two that you just made. They simply would never have occurred to me. How can I learn to think like that about my own teaching?"

This colleague had correctly spotted that I was not offering a programmatic solution but an invitation to a way of thinking that could reorient our practice. He was also right to focus on a learning process. None of us come to questions about faith and teaching as blank slates or with pristine perception. We are frequently too busy for sustained reflection on the details of what we do, and our culture has already offered us convenient mental templates to work from. Christian beliefs are for devotions and the state of our soul, a common template suggests, and faith is a personal matter. Teaching, on the other hand, is efficient routine, a pragmatic matter of getting to standardized outcomes with as little disruption as possible.[1] Wrestling with the intersection, grasping faith as a way of leaning into the whole of life and teaching as a faith-infused endeavor, can feel like trying to engage an unfamiliar muscle that will complain for days afterward. Even if we are entirely willing, the moves can feel awkward. How do we learn to think about faith and teaching in the same breath without things turning weird?

I am not sure exactly what I said in reply. The context, with three minutes left to offer a response, seemed to call for a compact strategy, a quick plan for solving the difficulty. I didn't have one. I still don't, and I don't think that's how it works. I think that shaping and reshaping our pedagogy requires attentiveness over time, repeated engagements, and incremental connections, not just a sudden epiphany or a tidy and timeless framework. I think that what we should be seeking along the way is patterns of practice that are plausible extensions of what we believe, not unique Christian techniques. Learning to think faith and teaching together is a pilgrim road.

This book is my response to that seminar question. It is about living into the habits of reflection that might help us to more fluently trace the patterns of faith in the fabric of our teaching. I hope it speaks to those who teach in a range of settings, faith-based or otherwise. I intend the book to echo the biblical invitation to love "not . . . with words or tongue, but with actions and in truth" (1 John 3:18).[2] As my university's namesake John Calvin put it, Christianity is "not a doctrine of the tongue, but of life" and "will be unprofitable if it does not change our heart, pervade our manners, and transform us into new creatures."[3] I hope that the book will help educators to think of the truth as lodged in pedagogical actions, not just in opportunities (valuable as they are) to pray or state a Christian idea in class. I aim to approach the matter gradually, stride by stride along the journey through a teaching semester.

I will not be building a case here that we should think of teaching as something that can be Christian; that was the burden of a previous book. In *On Christian Teaching*, I argued that thinking about whether education is Christian must include reflection on how faith shapes pedagogy.[4] Neither a view of pedagogy as neutral technique nor a view of it as a quest for a unique set of Christian moves can in the end do justice to the complex fabric of teaching. Our way of teaching creates a kind of temporary home, with specific contours and rhythms, in which we invite students to dwell and grow. A Christian approach to this is not just a matter of whether Christian character is modeled, Christian prayers are prayed, or Christian things are said and discussed. The process of teaching is not just a routine of efficient methods. The pedagogical choices that we make when we shape teaching and learning are sufficiently value-laden that it makes sense to ask how being Christian might contribute to shaping them. There is no way to derive the one right way to teach from the pages of the New Testament, nor can faith statements replace careful investigation of how learning works. Yet the choices, hunches, and habits that shape our teaching arise from and project a web of meaning. They tell a story about our beliefs and values, whether we teach in a Christian school or not. We can work toward ways of teaching that are consistent with and are plausible extensions of our Christian commitments, connecting what our faith helps us to see with how we engage our students and how we support that engagement with the details of daily practice.[5]

This way of approaching the matter rubs up against the powerful modern instinct to see teaching as value-free technique whose sole purpose is to produce gains in measurable learning outcomes. Techniques and measurement have their place. Yet in teaching, as in many other kinds of human connection, reducing the matter to technique risks denaturing the very process we set out to enhance. Learners are not objects. When we teach, we help shape how they relate to one another and to the wider world; we create emphases and silences; we structure the flow of time; we include and exclude, approve and reject, show and hide, judge and bless. All of this implicitly tells students who we are and who they are supposed to be. All of it becomes part of our educational responsibility, part of what we helped make happen. As Parker Palmer puts it: "I must take responsibility for my mediator role, for the way my mode of teaching exerts a slow but steady formative pressure on my students' sense of self and world. I teach more than a body of knowledge or a set of skills. I teach a mode of relationship between the knower and the known, a way of being in the world."[6]

If we aspire to a Christ-oriented life, we need to reflect on what that means for the how of teaching, not because being Christian gives us a magic shortcut to correct technique or a unique set of moves, but because how we teach shapes the values and rhythms of the formative pedagogical home into which we invite students.[7] We are responsible for the stories we tell, the patterns we create, the homes we make.

Such was, in brief outline, the argument of *On Christian Teaching*. That book was an attempt to show with examples how it can be meaningful to think of the teaching process as informed and shaped by faith. I was offering a case that thinking of teaching choices as plausible extensions of Christian convictions makes sense.

In this book I take it as a given that we can and should connect faith and pedagogy. Here I focus more on how we move forward from that premise. Suppose we are persuaded that teaching choices and faith commitments are intertwined. Suppose we conceive a desire to better fit the ways we shape learning to our convictions about the life of the world. Suppose we want to get better at thinking about faith and teaching together. What then? What does the road look like, and how do we walk it wisely? If we'd like to be a pilgrim, how do we make progress?

PILGRIM PRACTICES

"How can I learn to think like that?" If I heard the question right, it was more about the journey than the map. I don't think the questioner was fishing for a better philosophical summary of how faith is supposed to relate to learning, with everything assigned its proper place. The need was more for a way of growing into practical wisdom, gaining a facility in tracing connections between faith and teaching that do not feel forced, weird, or coercive. It was a matter of getting better at spotting chances for wholeness and defter at walking into them.[1] What might I be able to offer within the confines of a book to help with that need?

Mark Jordan writes, "We don't need books about teaching so much as books that teach."[2] I hope that this book falls into both categories. One of the things we are learning about learning from cognitive scientists is that we get better at the thing we practice, and not necessarily at the thing we think we are doing.[3] For instance, active thinking and recall are better for learning than passive reading. Repeatedly reading over our notes before a test gives us practice at reading information rather than recalling it, which is unfortunate if what we wanted to get better at was recalling the information during the test. Finding some way of making ourselves repeatedly try to remember the material (such as quizzing with a partner) and actively thinking it through is a much better strategy if the thing we want to get better at is recall.[4] There also seems to be evidence that generating explanations for what we have just read and spacing out our learning, with ideas interleaving over time, can help our learning processes.[5]

There are some kinds of knowledge that we need in the background if we want to get better at connecting faith and teaching. We need enough theological understanding and biblical literacy for the faith element to amount to more than random Bible verses or vaguely noble sentiments. We need enough understanding of how teaching and learning work to be able to spot the possibilities. But if the thing we want to get better at is making faith-teaching connections, we need repeated practice at noticing and actively thinking through those connections. This is not the kind of learning that can be conveyed in a neat set of distinctions that show where all the pieces go. It is the kind of learning that comes through repeated movement back and forth between conviction and practice while actively seeking to figure out how each might lead us to modify our grasp of the other. This kind of learning is the core focus of this book. The book does not offer a theory of faith and teaching, a unique set of teaching strategies, or a guide to all the ways in which teaching can be Christian. It offers repeated practice at noticing and thinking through ways in which faith and the process of teaching might connect in everyday practice.

I have therefore organized the book not around principles but around moments and examples. The main divisions are built around the mundane procession of moments that all teachers experience every semester. Starting the course. Setting some norms for interaction. Choosing how to frame the material. Assigning tasks. Repeating things. Pausing. Bringing things to a close. The topics are deliberately ordinary. The shape of our teaching is mainly built from the unspectacular, ongoing choices and actions that gradually shape the texture of life in the classroom. If we are going to think well about Christian faith and teaching, we have to learn to reflect well on those ordinary steps in the journey. They are good places to focus precisely because they happen all the time.

Each main part is divided into several chapters that focus on examples of ways of beginning, repeating, pausing, and so on. These examples are not "best practices," at least if that implies the best way to do things everywhere. They are not attempts to describe unique Christian behaviors that no one else could inhabit. They do not cover every relevant Christian belief. The point of each is that it shows an attempt to trace connections between some kind of Christian conviction and some everyday practice of teaching and learning. The examples are there to provide concrete ways into reflecting on how faith can inform teaching. They are intended more as a workout than as a recipe.

Some of the examples are drawn from higher education classrooms, some are drawn from elementary school or secondary school contexts.

Wherever and whatever you teach, you will find many examples that are not directly from your setting. The goal is not necessarily for you to mimic the examples but to reflect on what is going on in them. Each example narrative is followed by reflective exercises that invite you to think through the connections that have been made and the further connections you might make. The first ones are at the end of this chapter. I do not aim to do all the work for you; that would defeat the purpose. If you decide that you would have made the connections differently, that may be a perfectly good outcome if it helps you to think through your own teaching in your context in ways that bear good fruit. Instead of approaching the examples and exercises with the question, "Can I copy this activity as is in my own classroom?," I invite you to approach them with questions like, "Does this example help me to see possible ways for faith to inform my teaching practices?" and "How might this kind of connection be made in my context or at my level of teaching?"

The examples chosen here do not for the most part focus on openly devotional moments or moments in which Christian ideas are discussed in class. They are not centered on praying in class, or leading devotions, or bringing the Bible into learning. Those things are well worth thinking about and learning to do well, and I touch on them here and there, but in this book I focus on what is going on when we are just teaching our subject material, even if we are not in a setting in which openly religious discourse would be appropriate or welcome. Talking persuasively about Christian beliefs and praying together are important, but they are not what most Christian teachers are doing most of the time. Mostly, we are teaching other things, managing the moment, trying to help students learn, and planning a path through our week.

I suspect that the most fruitful way to use this book might be to read one of the chapters, think about the exercises, go try something in your classroom, attend to what happens, discuss it with a colleague, and then come back for another chapter. You are, of course, welcome to graze through the whole text and then go back to the most promising bits. There are benefits to reading parts in the context of wholes, and there are some recurring themes. However you tackle it, the kind of learning I have in mind is the kind that builds reflective habits and is embodied in developing practices, a pilgrimage of steady, iterative formation. As William James put it over a hundred years ago, our learning becomes well integrated into our being through "the same thing recurring on different days, in different contexts, read, recited on, referred to again and again, related to other things and reviewed."[6]

No doubt there can be benefits to starting on the mountaintop, with big theological or philosophical ideas. I am not rejecting other approaches, just trying out this one. One liability of starting from the big picture is that we are all too often left no closer to knowing what to do on Tuesday morning in class. Here I focus on the meaning of what happens in class. Faith is not just for the moment when we get to stop the traffic and do something that only Christians could do. The teaching process itself is not innocent, but a way of shaping a learning home that carries formative impulses for teacher and learner. I invite you to join me in the experiment of starting from "assigning," or "pausing," or "repeating," and looking out for how faith might be in play. I hope that in doing so, we can inch closer to habitually noticing the faith-informed fabric of our ordinary, everyday choices.

"Come, child! Learn to be wise."

Exercises

- What steps have you already taken to grow your understanding of how faith and teaching intersect? Where do you most sense a need for growth?
- Make a plan for how you are going to tackle this book. How will you space out the reading so that you can follow through on the exercises that follow each chapter? What is a pace that can realistically sustain reflection amid the existing demands of your schedule?
- Read and reflect on Psalm 25 at least three times this week on different days. Notice verses 4–5:

  Show me Your ways, O LORD;
  Teach me Your paths.
  Lead me in Your truth and teach me" (NKJV),

  and the echo in verses 8–10:

He teaches sinners in the way.
The humble He guides in justice,
And the humble He teaches His way.
All the paths of the LORD are mercy and truth. (NKJV)

Look at the range of words associated here with teaching. What picture of teaching is suggested? How does it connect with the picture of teaching in the illustration at the beginning of this book? How is your ability to humbly notice mercy, justice, and truth in the world around you important for the kind of teacher you become? Look for a chance to discuss your thoughts with a colleague.

BEGINNING

THE COURAGE TO BEGIN

For teachers, beginning is unavoidable. The first class happens, ready or not. We can't put it off until we have done a little more preparation or acquired a little more virtue. It happens again and again, with a fresh topic or new students.

How we begin is eloquent. In the first minutes and hours of a teaching sequence, we provide learners with a vision (explicit and implicit) of what lies ahead. We communicate (consciously and unconsciously) what we think learning is, what we care about most, and who we want learners to be. The way we begin preaches who we are and what we hope for.

I have a bemused admiration for the way Bernard of Clairvaux began his extensive series of sermons on the Song of Songs. Bernard, an influential Cistercian abbot, started writing the sermons in 1135 and left them incomplete at his death in 1153. It is unclear whether they were ever actually preached. In the opening sermon he plays repeatedly with the image of teaching as breaking bread.[1]

The image appears early in the sermon. Drawing on New Testament imagery, Bernard orients his hearers to what is to come with an exhortation.[2] "Be ready then to feed on bread rather than milk," he writes. "Solomon has bread to give that is splendid and delicious, the bread of that book called The Song of Songs. Let us bring it forth then, if you please, and break it."[3]

Consider the context. Bernard describes previous teaching on Proverbs and Ecclesiastes as "two loaves of which it has been your pleasure to taste"[4] and now announces more delicious bread to come. The new loaf, the series on Song of Songs, will be chewed on so assiduously that eighty-six sermons later he will have reached the first verse of the third chapter. The last seven sermons are devoted to that single verse, so who knows how many more would have been needed to reach the end of the book. Perhaps he was such a charismatic teacher that his monks were eager for whatever he taught next, but I can't help wondering whether he could really count on a universal expectation of bliss.

This is why his comment about delicious bread makes me smile. Other opening gambits might seem more practical. Perhaps: "This is going to test your patience, but if you hang in there, it can help you grow." Or maybe: "This might not be your favorite thing to do next, but we can get through this together and gain from it." Instead, he announces something wonderful: "Solomon has bread to give that is splendid and delicious." He invites his hearers to think of themselves as people about to feast on good food. Even acknowledging that writing this may have been easier than saying it while looking his monks in the eye, I suspect that this kind of beginning requires a little courage. I can't help admiring his nerve. If we start a lengthy, demanding, and excruciatingly detailed class by telling our students how delicious it will be, and we intend the comment to be taken as sincere, we have given ourselves a lot to live up to. I wonder how many of us could make such a claim without irony, or at least a little trepidation.

Is he just boasting? It's possible, though it's not the most charitable assumption. Bernard does not ground his claim to future delight in his own powers of entertainment or his special teaching gifts. Instead, he leads with the conviction that what he has to teach is precious. Solomon has prepared something delicious for us. This text is profoundly worth exploring. It will reward our attention and nourish our souls.

After placing Solomon before our mind's eye, Bernard emphasizes that he is only in a derivative and secondary sense the teacher:

> The Master of the house is present, it is the Lord you must see in the breaking of the bread. For who else could more fittingly do it? It is a task that I would not dare to arrogate to myself. So look upon me as one from whom you look for nothing. For I myself am one of the seekers, one who begs along with you for the food of my soul, the nourishment of my spirit. . . . O God most kind, break your bread for this hungering flock, through my hands indeed if it should please you, but with an efficacy that is all your own.[5]

Like the pilgrim teacher in the image that started this book, he signals explicitly that he does not have in himself everything his learners need. The source of life and truth is somewhere beyond him. Yet he also communicates confidence that Christ will take the bread that is broken in the classroom through the act of teaching and turn it into nourishment. He offers this as a hope for his students to share. Christ is present in the teaching and the learning, transforming them into a sacred meal in the presence of God.

A Starting Stance

I don't think the best takeaway here is that we should all start class by talking about bread, or even necessarily by enthusing about the beauty of what we have in store for our students. My point here is not to call for stirring motivational speeches, or to offer the best opening line, or to claim that everything on every syllabus can with a straight face be sold as scintillating. What Bernard is modeling is not the jolly overconfidence of the advertising jingle. I am more interested in examining the posture that we display in our opening words and gestures, and how it can be rooted in our faith.

If the way we begin communicates who we are and what we hope for, what messages are students receiving from us at the outset? What can they glean about how we imagine them and their needs and capacities? What might they sense about whether we think of ourselves as beside them on the road, or looming over them, or disappointed by them? What do we state or imply about the point of learning, about what counts as success and why we should care? I suspect that many students have tentative answers to all these questions quite early in the semester, perhaps already on the first day.

Bernard's opening models a settled faith in the beauty and necessity of learning, in the existence of truth that can nourish us, and in God's desire to be present in our learning. I suspect that this faith is directly supported by the way it leans on biblical language; left to our own resources, it is easy to begin teaching with less serene confidence. From faith comes the hope that good will follow. Faith and hope underpin the courage to announce that what follows will feed us if we can muster the maturity to approach it with expectancy rather than cynicism. ("Unless in vain you have prolonged your study of divine teaching," he allows in a provocative aside.)[6] The language of breaking bread together suggests a context of mutual love.

Bernard's imagery offers his students an initial lens through which to interpret the tasks that lie ahead of them. The opening rhetorical frame is not focused on grades, productivity, being smart, competitiveness, or personal success. Like other framing metaphors, the image of breaking bread together creates a kind of accountability.[7] It promises that what the teacher prepares each week will be bread (genuinely nourishing), not cake (entertaining but nutritionally hollow). It suggests a hospitable stance toward students and an inclusive classroom culture; Bernard asks us to think of "the friend who comes to us on his travels," who might join the meal and will need to receive what is taught as coming "from the cupboard of a friend."[8] It invites a willingness to actively chew on solid food, not milk, and to be attentive to one another's needs as we do so, so that some do not overeat while others go away hungry. Teacher and students might succeed or fail at any of this, but the opening image tells a story about what we should hope for and therefore what we should work for together.

Of course, Bernard was teaching theology in a monastery, and most of us are not. I suggest that this difference is an invitation rather than a barrier. Perhaps the welcome that we articulate at the beginning of our course will be less overtly and much less elaborately theological, and that may be entirely appropriate. Perhaps we will lean on different metaphors. After all, in the opening chapters of this book we have already played with images of pilgrim journeys and sacred meals; there is no single best image.[9] Yet we can approach our beginnings, big and small, with some of the same questions in mind. How might we communicate that there is truth and beauty to explore, and that they are a gracious gift from beyond ourselves? How might we communicate a proper humility regarding our own role in that exploration? How might we invite students into a way of learning together that fosters care for one another and calls for virtues as well as intellect? And where will we find the courage that might make such a beginning imaginable?

Exercises

- Compare the image of learning as shared pilgrimage in the introduction and the image of teaching as breaking bread in this chapter. How are they similar and different? What Christian ideas does each image pull into focus? What aspects of the learning process does each image invite us to notice? Spend some time reflecting on this and make notes under the prompts "If teaching is like a pilgrimage, then . . ." and "If teaching is like breaking bread, then . . ."
- With which opening words do you typically begin a course or semester? What do they imply about your vision of learning and student growth? Write them down to gain some critical distance, then share them with a colleague for their reaction. Ask some of your students for their impressions of how classes typically begin at your school and what they infer from that beginning about what the school values.
- What kind of support and encouragement do you need to be able to begin the semester with humble confidence? Write down some specific ways you could offer the same support and encouragement to your colleagues. Choose one and commit to acting on it in the coming week.

NAMING NAMES

We approach a new course or semester with some hopes for how our students will grow. At some point, often before the first class meeting, the general idea of "students" turns into the specific human beings who are going to be entrusted to us. A vague category turns into names and faces, each representing a person who will learn with us. Learning those names and faces becomes one of our first practical challenges.

In a thoughtful article about learning names at the start of a course, Jacob Stratman invites us to think carefully about the kind of encounter with students that we are seeking.[1] Stratman takes his starting point from Zygmunt Bauman's account of three ways in which human beings can come together: being-aside, being-with, and being-for.[2]

In being-aside, other people are just objects in the background. They are part of the space that we move through, but as soon as we have registered their presence and coordinates, our attention glides away from them and they become part of the backdrop. Think of the other people sitting in a café where you are reading a book. In some thin sense they are in your company, but they are at the margins of your concerns.

Sometimes we shift to being-with. We pick out background figures and shift our attention to them, and they become less like scenery. In Bauman's words, they are "made into persons" as we turn to them for some kind of encounter.[3] Nevertheless, our connection with them remains confined within the duration of the encounter. Most of their self and most of our self remain hidden. The interaction has little or no consequence for our future lives, and once it is over we no longer need to know one another.[4] Think of the person at the next table in the café whom you ask to lend you a pen, or the waiter who asks if you need anything. As Bauman puts it, "no more of the self tends to be deployed in the encounter than the topic-at-hand demands; and no more of the other is highlighted than the topic-at-hand permits."[5] We let just as much of ourselves show as is needed to get the transaction done, no more.

Sometimes we discover the possibility of being-for. Here the focus is not on prescribed roles, but on the persons themselves. We each bring who we are and we are open to being affected by one another. We exist for each other in richer, more morally engaged ways. Think of a conversation struck up with someone in a café that opens into serious discussion followed by plans to meet again. The encounter impacts both parties and generates future connections and consequences. We enter into this kind of encounter "for the sake of safeguarding and defending the uniqueness of the Other."[6] In other words, the other person matters to us not just because of their function (pen owner, waiter) and their ability to do what we want, but because they are a unique person in their own right, with their own ideas, potential, and worth.

How do we encounter students, and how do students encounter their teachers in school? Some classes, such as those occurring in large lecture halls, may never move past being-aside. One student from a large university recently told me she did not believe any of her professors knew her name or would recognize her if they met her outside class.

Stratman worries that even when we move beyond being-aside, our classrooms may be too exclusively focused on being-with. Students and teachers play their scripted roles, information is communicated, transactions are completed, assignments are exchanged for grades, but moral engagement and transformation remain unlikely. He wonders whether "teachers, through a variety of small gestures, can carry a posture of recognition, through which moments of 'being-for' could predominate in the classroom experience instead of the typical, conventional 'being-with.'"[7]

Stratman envisions approaching a semester with a determined hope that significant human connection can occur and that deep change might follow.[8] Hope is neither certain prediction nor blind optimism. There are other forces in play than our intentions, and things might not turn out well. We cannot guarantee transformative encounters by getting the techniques right. But beginning from hope can keep us from foreclosing on the possibilities before we get under way.

Small Gestures

How does hope translate into small gestures? Stratman focuses on one small gesture that is part of his preparation for class. He obtains the class list as far ahead of the semester as possible (at his institution it includes both names and pictures) and uses it to begin shaping his own posture toward his students. He writes, "Part of my spiritual and pedagogical preparation for the class is praying for them as individual students and for them as a class, as well as praying for me and my preparations. I must admit that a more recent practice, thanks to discussions with colleagues, is to contact my classes before the semester begins to ask them to pray for me, their classmates, and for the semester, so that the ideas connected with recognition are not merely one-way. I need to be recognized by them as much as they need to be recognized by me."[9] Prayer changes the process of learning names from a mechanical challenge into a spiritual discipline. It expresses hope for the teacher's transformation, not just that of the students. The emphasis shifts from how to manage students to how teacher and students alike can begin to live into mutual recognition.

Stratman reports several benefits for his teaching. The most immediate benefit is to consciously shift his focus from his own task list to students' well-being. Prayer for students is a way of leaning into being-for, consciously approaching his students as people he will serve and know rather than tasks he will manage. A prayerful beginning positions him differently and lets him see his students differently. It serves as a way of fostering a "hospitable disposition in the teacher before class commences."[10] Prayer nurtures the realization that he is "not the center of the relationship, nor the creator of the subject of study."[11]

Further, prayer "tends to bridge the distance" between instructor and students, because whether students know it or not, his relationship with them "started to take shape weeks prior to [the] initial meeting."[12] The initial investment in prayer means that the teacher knows most of the students' names before the first class begins and has begun to see each student as a person and to desire good things for them individually. This has already begun to erode the initial sense of distance from the teacher's point of view.

Stratman's account rings true to me at this point. I have observed a similar effect in myself from intentional pre-semester practices. I aim to meet with each student individually at the very beginning of the semester with the goal of hearing them talk about their learning experiences and their hopes and goals for the class. During the COVID pandemic, I added to my pre-semester practices an outdoor ice cream social so that we could see one another's faces before learning with masks in place. Sometimes, like Stratman, I have used the photo directory as a prayer guide. I hope that these interventions help students to find their way into the semester, but I am also conscious of the benefits for me. When I walk into the classroom, it is with a sense of encountering people whom I already know just a little. This has a discernible effect on my teaching. I tend to be a little more relaxed, less anxious, less liable to fall back into preoccupation with myself or trying to come across as impressive. I aim to turn my students as quickly as possible from names on a list or parts of an environment to be managed into people I know. To the degree that I can close this gap, it becomes more likely that I will teach students well and build fruitful connections with them. On occasions when I have been overwhelmed with things to do and have skimped on these initial preparations, I have noticed a difference and regretted the slower curve toward connection.

Stratman notes that when class does begin, conventional student expectations are disrupted at the outset. Students are used to arriving in class as strangers, unsure what kind of regard they will receive from the teacher. Stratman describes in the words of his own students the common anxiety felt when entering a new class and confronting a new teacher, a new schedule, a new classroom culture. His pre-semester discipline enables him to greet students by name in the hallway and welcome them into the learning space, creating a moment of recognition.[13] Instead of just being students, those who enter the class are now persons with names.

There is some empirical evidence to support the idea that students' perception that a teacher knows their name can have positive effects on their attitudes to learning.[14] Yet Stratman's main focus here is ethical rather than strategic. Given what he believes about learners as made in God's image and the classroom as a hospitable space, he focuses on the kind of welcome his students should experience as class begins.

I was recently privileged to read the reflections of a student at my own university on a class that she had experienced earlier in her program. Her comments about the instructor echo Stratman's central concern:

> When we arrived on the first day of class, [the instructor] remembered each of our names. Throughout the course, he remembered details about our lives and was intentional about asking us follow-up questions for big, tragic, or exciting events. I'm thankful to have had many educators throughout my educational experience who I felt cared about me, but he was the first one who took an interest in me as a human, not just as his student.[15]

The way we prepare for the start of class reveals how we are thinking about our students. The way we shape the first encounter sketches the first contours of the pedagogical home that we will share as learning begins in earnest. Our faith is in play even before class starts.

Exercises

- The first half of this chapter describes Stratman's debt to Bauman's account of types of social encounters. The second half focuses more directly on how Stratman's faith is guiding his practice. What specific Christian beliefs and practices does he explicitly mention? From what wider Christian convictions about people and relationships does he seem to implicitly draw? What changes in his practice resulted from these Christian points of reference?
- What are you typically feeling at the beginning of the first class of the semester? How does this affect how you teach? What are your strategies for decreasing preoccupation with your own anxieties or status and increasing your ability to focus on your students' presence and needs? Invite a trusted colleague or friend for coffee and discuss these questions in light of this chapter.
- For at least one of your current class groups, start an intentional and prayerful practice of focusing on the students as persons. This could take various forms. You could, for instance, use the class list or seating plan as a focus for prayer, intentionally ask individual students about their day, pray for a different student each day in rotation, or something else. Keep the scale of your time investment modest and realistic so that the practice is sustainable. Share with a colleague any changes you perceive in your experience of teaching.

GOALS, COVENANTS, AND HOPE

The courses I teach are accompanied by written syllabi, which means their goals are communicated in writing. If your courses do not use syllabi, that's OK; what I say about syllabi in this chapter applies to other ways of communicating initial expectations to students. The focus remains on looking for how faith is linked to teaching. Whether you use a syllabus or not, ask yourself: What moves are being made here? How could they have been different? Why?

Covenantal Syllabi

Quentin Schultze, in his helpful volume on servant teaching, comments that one of his goals when writing a course syllabus is "to capture covenantal practices for mutual responsibility and care." He adds: "I want students to know specifically what's required of them. But I also want them to know what's required of me . . . [the syllabus is] a description of community practices with mutual understandings as well as obligations."[1] Conceived this way, a syllabus becomes more like a covenant than a broadcast. It describes the normative shape of the class's life together and requires engagement from both sides.

At the beginning of a semester, Schultze provides the syllabus to students ahead of time with a request for their feedback. When classes start, he sets aside some time to discuss responses to the syllabus. The focus is not so much on making sure students have noted the deadlines and reading schedule as it is on whether the syllabus as written will help the class to function well as a community. Examples of questions discussed include: "Will my approach to testing and grading reduce anxiety and enhance learning? Are there better alternatives? What about the schedule, given everything else happening on campus during the key dates for exams and submissions? How should we help a classmate who must miss one or more sessions? Would someone be willing to audio record class sessions for absent students or those who wish to relisten? Should students encourage one another to share lecture or reading notes, or even to form study groups?"[2] Once the syllabus is firmly in place, any subsequent changes are subjected to a student ballot. Schultze recommends viewing a syllabus less as a list of impositions and penalties and more as a common rule for living together, similar in its more limited fashion to the rules of life used in the monastic tradition.

I like the idea of thinking of course syllabi as covenantal and as common rules for life together. Framing the matter like this pushes us away from posting declarations for students to read or ignore and toward a culture of mutual responsibility. That does not imply giving up our authority to shape the class, our right to insist on certain points, or our expertise in designing a learning sequence. It means that authority and expertise are put to work within a visible posture of service and a framework of mutual obligation.

The exchange that happens around the syllabus may be the most important element here, especially since the evidence is mixed at best regarding the effect of syllabus design alone on student perceptions.[3] The syllabus provides a shared text to ground the exchange. The syllabus *and* how it is communicated point to the shape of the intended pedagogical home in which teacher and students are to live.

Syllabi and Accountability

At the beginning of the global pandemic, many of us were plunged into Zoom-meeting free fall, even if we had rarely (or never) taught online. As we faced the challenge of suddenly designing online versions of courses with no notice, there was a need for quick and ready tools that could keep us moving. One such tool quickly shared with faculty at my university was a sample online course syllabus. It helped me formulate syllabi for my own courses, but it also made moves that I felt I needed to change.

The sample syllabus focused noticeably on individual success and quantity of participation. It did refer to how students' posts on discussion boards could help broaden their classmates' perspectives. More prominent, however, was a focus on how posting regularly online could contribute to "your success" and offer a chance to share and refine "your ideas." Of three assessment criteria named, one focused on thoughtful reflection, while two were about frequency of posting and following instructions correctly. The whole gave me the impression that what counted was diligent rule following and individual performance. That was not quite the conversation that I wanted to have with my students.

The shared university template has evolved significantly after more mature reflection and discussion, though the early draft did push me to reflect on what I most wanted to discuss with students at the beginning of the semester. Here is part of one of my own attempts at a syllabus statement for an education class:

> Learning to think deeply entails paying attention to and learning from those around us. The best teaching does not grow out of solitary reflection. This course will therefore include an emphasis on collaboration. Success means not just getting your own tasks done but helping those around you to become better learners and teachers, so that more of the needs of their future students will be met. This is an important way in which you can begin to serve those students now as well as honor the gifts and needs that each other participant in IDIS 357 brings to the class. As we work at collaborating on transformative educational practices, we will have opportunities to try to do *justice to* the ideas of others, exercise *patience with* their learning process, [and] offer our own ideas with *humility* (which means not thinking too highly of ourselves but also being willing to share ideas openly). Our goal is not to win arguments. It is to figure out how teaching languages can be a work of love.

With a paragraph such as this, I am aiming to shift the center of gravity toward our responsibilities to one another and the virtues that we should work on as we learn together. I want to frame learning practices as a form of care for others, an impulse that arises from Christian reflection on how I should view human relationships (see CONNECTING). I want to show how that will inform what I am looking for in student work. I hope to provide initial guidance that can resonate with Schultze's "rule of life" approach.

I want the emphasis on mutually supportive community to be consistent across the different learning practices described in various sections of the syllabus. Here is how I describe the reading assignments on another class syllabus:

> Each week you will read scholarly work on curriculum and instruction. There is a long tradition of Christian reflection on what it means to read in light of the calling to love God and neighbor. The author of each text we read and your fellow readers are all neighbors. Each time we engage with a thoughtful work we have an opportunity to grow in our practice of *justice* (can I read carefully enough to fairly represent what the author is aiming to say, and not overlay it with my own prejudices or distort it through hasty judgments?), *patience* (when a text seems wrong or difficult or irrelevant, can I give it time to unfold and wait to find the point of connection?), *humility* (can I come to each text looking for what I can learn from it and not stand too quickly in judgment over it?) and *charity* (can I read in such a way as to believe well of the author for as long as possible?). This is far from easy. It means resisting the temptation to treat thoughtful texts as sources of quick information snippets or fodder for winning arguments. I will be looking for evidence in your forum discussions of how you have been reading.

Obviously, this paragraph includes language that implies a shared Christian context, though the emphases could still be expressed in other words in contexts where the overtly theological language might be problematic. Again, the idea here is not that wording the syllabus in a particular way makes a major difference on its own. In fact, the reasons for paying attention to the matter start with me. Care taken with the syllabus pushes me to explicitly articulate some of the deep hopes that inform my course planning. If I then use it as a basis for conversation with students, I can communicate expectations and promises more thoughtfully than if I attempt to do so off the cuff.[4] In the paragraph above, I hope to communicate to students that reading can be an intentional practice within which we can work out our calling to study in ways consistent with love of God and neighbor. Articulating this in the syllabus helps me clarify my hopes for the course and creates a shared reference point for ongoing discussion and accountability.

Acknowledging shared responsibility means that less burden is placed on the syllabus document per se. The syllabus is not a onetime declaration that students must remember to obey. It provides shared language for acknowledging when we fall short and discussing how to grow in our practices. It will be followed by assignments that explicitly require students to reflect on our approach to reading.[5] There will be short extracts from authors across the centuries who have sought to articulate how Christians might read. There will be opportunities for reflective journaling, and exercises designed to focus students on their reading process and not just their reading coverage. Such later moves provide chances to keep the hopes expressed in the syllabus before our eyes.

My syllabus paragraph implicitly promises (not least through the "we" language) that the vision described will inform my own approach to the course. The exercise is as much about my own accountability as it is about requirements for students; the syllabus becomes in a certain sense my conscience in relation to a particular course. The hopes named in the syllabus make me accountable to provide a supportive infrastructure for their realization, and to seek to model this kind of reading in my own handling of texts, both assigned texts and those authored by students during the course. I must reflect on how my teaching practices (assignments, assessments, verbal habits) might help, or whether they nudge students toward skim reading and quick searches for answers.[6] If the virtue language is to be more than top-down moralizing, it must commit me to walking the same road as my students as we engage with texts together.

Naming an envisioned pedagogical home through a shared rule of life entails planning for practices that might sustain the life of that home. A careful rule of life matters not because the document does all the work, but because it helps us to know who we are trying to become together. Reflecting on the hopes that should inform the syllabus for a particular course can be a discipline that pushes me toward public commitment to the beliefs underpinning my approach to learning.

Exercises

- Look back over this chapter and list the specific connections made between course planning and explicit or implicit Christian beliefs. Don't just look for theology words; look also for places where a stated value seems to be rooted in a Christian concern. Then review your own planning practices and list the specific hopes and beliefs that inform your expectations for students. What resonances and differences do you find between the two lists?

- If your classes do not use a written syllabus, how else might you make your hopes for your students a matter of shared public record to which you can refer back as the semester progresses? How might you invite students into a shared rule of life?
- The example at the end of this chapter focuses on reading practices. Draft a similar paragraph that focuses on another basic learning practice (e.g., writing, listening, lab work, discussing) and names the virtues you seek in and through that practice. Adjust the language to fit your context. Then list a few examples of learning practices and activities that might arise from seeking to teach in a way consistent with your paragraph. Share the results with a colleague and a student for feedback, asking them especially whether the teaching strategies seem to fit the stated hopes.

STARTING THE STORY

It is good to spend time choosing a way of framing the semester, steering your heart toward your students, and preparing a thoughtful statement of intent. But at some point we have to start learning some subject matter. There will be a first topic, a first heading, a first picture that students encounter in class. The way the teaching sequence begins is another implicit proposal for how we will learn together, so let's look at some examples of starting points.[1]

Rewind

This book began, appropriately enough, with an example of a beginning. My opening image was from the first page of a language textbook. I wonder if you remember the first class you took in a language other than your mother tongue, and how it began. What were the first topic, the first conversation, and the first image? If you can't recall, how would you expect a language textbook to begin?

The image I used was taken from the most famous language textbook in the history of Western education, the *Orbis Sensualium Pictus* by John Amos Comenius.[2] This text enjoyed enormous international success across several centuries, with at least 248 editions published between 1658 and the mid-twentieth century.[3] It is often called the first picture book for children. This is false, however; the use of pictures in primers of various kinds started centuries earlier. But it was a major development in the systematic use of images in schools.[4]

The opening image invited us to reflect on the connections between intellectual, moral, and spiritual formation and the pilgrimage toward responsibility and service on which teacher and learner are to travel together. Comenius argued that education needed to address three basic human capacities: our desire to understand, our need to learn how to virtuously handle the power that we have over others and our environment, and our need to delight in relating all things to God. "These three," he wrote, "are so intimately joined that no separation among them can be admitted, because in these the foundation of the present and the future life is established."[5] His understanding of humans as integrated intellectual/moral/spiritual beings needing help to grow into wisdom guided his choice of image for the first page. The rays of light, the path from darkness to service, the teacher's robe and staff, and the teacher's presence on the road with the student together tell a story about his vision of learning. The dialogue beneath the image positions the learner as a conversation partner, an asker of questions, and invites us toward wisdom. The beginning is a statement about the journey to come. The second chapter is simply titled "God."

Fast-Forward

What happens if we scroll forward into the next century? Prominent among the next generation of texts for learning Latin was *The London Vocabulary* by James Greenwood.[6] This book also did very well, with more than twenty-five editions over the course of the eighteenth and early nineteenth centuries. George Washington purchased a copy around 1765.[7] It borrows enough from the *Orbis Pictus* that it has sometimes been portrayed as basically an abridged imitation, yet its opening page launches a different story.

Though the opening picture in this text is more crowded, a number of elements have disappeared. Adam and Eve sit in the foreground, with the Hebrew name of God and some cherubs visible directly above them in the heavens. They are surrounded by a selection of creatures: animals, birds, fish, and celestial bodies. The rays of light from the sun, the moon, and God are now more explicitly distinguished. The talk of wisdom is gone, as are the pilgrim teacher, the darkness of sin, the path to virtue, the sense of a journey, the community in the background, and the accompanying dialogue. Now the opening chapter is headed "Of Things." The second chapter is titled "Of the Elements." Beneath the picture is a long list of nouns for the various kinds of things in the world. "God" and

THE LONDON VOCABULARY: OF THINGS

"angels" appear partway down the list. God still presides over the world, and there is still a distinct echo of the Genesis creation story, but the world is now more static, a large collection of objects.

In the *Orbis Pictus*, teacher and learner embark together on a vulnerable pilgrimage from sin and ignorance to wisdom.[8] In *The London Vocabulary*, humanity sits immobile, presiding at the center of an array of things. The text catalogues God in the midst of a list of nouns to be memorized, just one of the many things in the world. Future chapters will give us more catalogues of objects. The different starting points, like the opening scenes of different movies, begin to orient our imaginations toward different worlds that we will explore.

Fast-Forward Again

Suppose we skip a few centuries and catapult ourselves into the present day? On my office shelf, because I have used it multiple times to teach introductory German courses, sits the fifth edition of *Kontakte: A Communicative Approach*.[9] Comenius opened with an invitation to wisdom.

Greenwood opened with a list of things. How might our own social imaginary be different?

Chapter 1 of *Kontakte* is preceded by two preparatory introductions, which survey basic vocabulary for classroom objects and introduce simple sentence structures. The first full content chapter is titled "Who I Am and What I Do." The first major topic is now me. The first pictures in the chapter are cartoons of mostly young people engaging in leisure activities such as sailing, riding a horse, playing soccer, playing guitar, or ballet dancing.

The second chapter is titled "Possessions and Pleasures." How might I know who I am? Apparently by what I buy and what I like. In contrast to both the light-infused pilgrimage of the *Orbis Pictus* and the great collection of things in *The London Vocabulary*, we are now positioned at the center of our own consumer reality, surrounded by what we can own and enjoy. In place of creation, our own preferences and activities are appealed to as the foundation for what follows. If the first two texts seem quaintly historical, does this opening sound more like our kind of reality? Is this who we'd rather be? Once again, the way things get under way gives us clues about the kind of story that is supposed to frame our learning and living.

Subtraction Stories

Notice that the Christian question does not boil down to whether God is mentioned. It is true that the three books, in turn, affirm, marginalize, and banish divine agency. When the student asks in the opening dialogue in the *Orbis Pictus* who will help him gain wisdom, the teacher replies "I, with God."[10] God is still explicitly represented in the opening image of *The London Vocabulary*, yet God seems more distant, a thing to be named rather than an agent to be reckoned with. God is barely mentioned in *Kontakte*, appearing in stock phrases such as "thank God!" *Kontakte* generally maintains a conspicuous silence about religion. All of this is interesting, yet questions about faith and teaching do not stop there. It is not as if *Kontakte* would be telling the same story as the *Orbis Pictus* if only the God chapter were put back in or Bible verses were added to the pages. Adding God talk would not remove the story of individualistic consumerism told by the remaining material. It might even baptize it.[11] There is more to be interested in here from a Christian standpoint than the presence or absence of religious language.

Charles Taylor describes accounts of secularization that focus on the removal of religious frames of reference as "subtraction stories." He writes:

> I mean by this stories of modernity in general, and secularity in particular, which explain them by human beings having lost, or sloughed off, or liberated themselves from certain earlier, confining horizons, or illusions, or limitations of knowledge. What emerges from this process—modernity or secularity—is to be understood in terms of underlying features of human nature which were there all along, but had been impeded by what is now set aside. Against this kind of story, I will steadily be arguing that Western modernity, including its secularity, is the fruit of new inventions, newly constructed self-understandings and related practices, and can't be explained in terms of perennial features of human life.[12]

In other words, secularization was not just a matter of stripping away the God stuff and leaving behind the chapters on hobbies and food. It was a reimagining of who we are and how our world works, a repositioning of ourselves in a new story. If secularization is not just a matter of subtraction (e.g., removing the God chapter), then seeking a Christian way of inhabiting teaching and learning cannot be just a matter of addition (e.g., adding mentions of religion or prayers before class).

My point here is not, therefore, that the first lesson ought to be about God. Talking directly about theology at the very beginning might sometimes be the right move, or it might not be, depending on context, audience, subject area, and purpose. The point here is that whether we mention God right away or not, the way we begin is part of how our course tells a story about who we think we are and why we think we are learning. Even if our opening moves are not explicitly religious, they can be a better or a poorer fit with a Christian account of our place in the world as fallen image-bearers in need of reconciliation and transformation and called to lives of love.

Miroslav Volf argues that "at the heart of every good theology lies not simply a plausible intellectual vision but more importantly a compelling account of a way of life," and that our life practices (which include teaching and learning) "are Christian insofar as they are 'resonances' of God's engagement with the world."[13] Our curricular stories, whether or not they are directly about theology, may "resonate" to one degree or another with a vision of what animates God's engagement with the world. The way we begin sends signals about the kind of story we are going to tell. Those signals could, of course, prove to be thoroughly misleading, but that's another problem for another chapter. For now it will suffice to reflect on what trajectory students might glean from our opening moves.

Exercises

- If the point of this chapter is not that we should necessarily start out by mentioning God, summarize in your own words what it is saying about how being Christian relates to how we begin.
- Choose a course or sequence that you teach and identify the first image and the first topic heading that students will see. What might these suggest to students about what is important in the course, in the world, or in their own learning?
- For the same course or sequence, choose a different first image and topic heading, thinking about how they might connect to your overall vision for students' growth and the wider purpose for studying the material. Compare this beginning to the one you identified in the previous exercise—does either resonate more than the other with a Christian story about the world? Why/why not?

GATHERING FOR THE JOURNEY

I recently taught a new course for education students at Calvin University called "The Christian Teacher." I remarked to students early in the semester that teaching it was a vast opportunity for hypocrisy on my part. Teaching about teaching opens one's own teaching to scrutiny; adding the word "Christian" raises the stakes further.

My first challenge was figuring out how to begin. The beginning should create good initial momentum. It should position us well to start thinking about the core ideas in the course. While few, if any, teaching moves are uniquely Christian, the way we begin should be a plausible extension of Christian convictions. After some reflection, I settled on the following beginning. (It would only work in classes up to a certain size, but as usual my goal is not necessarily for you to copy it, but for you to think about what is happening.)

On the first morning, I moved the tables together so that we could sit in a single large circle. I sat down with the students as they trickled in. After introducing myself, I told them to pair up and ask their partner to share two interesting pieces of personal information that they were willing to have shared with the group. I then asked them to introduce their partner to the rest of us, using that information. As each pair completed their introductions, I quizzed the group cumulatively on what they had heard. I regularly referred us back to earlier introductions (do you remember the name of the person who likes running?) and drew attention to similarities and differences across the group (which three people have a cat?) as an aid to memory. This was easy at the beginning but took more work as more names and details were added.

After about twenty minutes, we all knew everyone's name and two things about each person. At that point I asked students to think back over what we had done and compare it to other class beginnings they had experienced. What choices had I made that could have been different? Had those choices influenced their perceptions of how this class was going to go? What messages did they take away from how other classes began? Could they already see any beliefs and values leaking through into my teaching, even in these opening minutes of the semester?

I was aiming for some of the same goods involved in another opening activity that I described at length in *On Christian Teaching*.[1] Within the first few minutes, each person got to speak in the relatively safe setting of a conversation with one other person, was heard, actively listened to others, had evidence that someone had listened to them, and was introduced by someone else into the group rather than having to manage that themselves. As usual, my goals were multiple. I wanted to free up cognitive space for learning by quickly addressing the anxieties most experience when beginning a new class with a crowd of strangers. I wanted to sow an expectation that we would focus on speaking our ideas and listening attentively to one another. I wanted to signal the value of each person present and lay some initial groundwork for talking later about Christian understandings of community and how they might relate to classrooms.[2] I wanted to signal that in a class about teaching, my own teaching moves would be as much part of the curriculum and fair game for critique as the ideas in lectures or readings. I wanted to work toward the realization that what at first felt like just a social icebreaker was already a way into the topic and expectations of the class.

That last point is one reason why I do not think there is one ideal way to start class. The opening minutes of class begin to communicate the value system that will shape learning interactions. The opening minutes should also connect coherently with the kind of learning that our course involves. These are not necessarily conflicting goals. With creative planning, our beginning can serve the subject we need to teach as well as the culture we want to create.

Some years ago, after leading professional development at a high school in another city, I found myself back in the area several months later for a conference. A teacher from the school approached me to tell me about how her semester had begun. "When you spoke to us," she recounted, "it was only a few days until the beginning of the new semester, but I knew I had to change my opening day." She had decided to rearrange her science course content so that she could open her first class with a visually dramatic experiment. She wanted to give learners a sense on the first day that science learning was going to be engaging and hands-on, and that there could be excitement in studying creation. As she told it, they made things explode on the first day. The effect was lasting. She recounted how her new opening seemed to have improved the way the students viewed her for the rest of the semester, even though the rest of her teaching was mostly unchanged. A perception was established at the beginning that this was an exciting class. Beginnings set baselines and trajectories that can affect the relational fabric and perceptions of the subject matter. They can function as a lens through which students interpret what is to follow.

Student Reflections

Following the first class of my education course, I asked students to journal about their wider experience of class beginnings and how it compared to the beginning we had just practiced. Their responses made fascinating reading as they described their reactions to various instructors' opening moves.

Some noticed that students were facing one another and that the professor was sitting among them at the start of our course. Both things stood out to them as different. They wrote of their dawning hunch that the instructor might be approachable, that, as they put it, the professor might be a human being. (I am not sure what other kind of being they might expect to lead a class, but the choice of words seems telling.) They contrasted this with classrooms in which, as Jasmine put it, "the placement of the people, desks, actions, and gestures showed that [the teacher] was the one with power and we were not."[3]

Several students described other classes that had begun with extended passivity on their part. Hannah wrote this: "One of my classes this semester began by going over the syllabus for the first thirty minutes of class with no introduction. I began to stress that this class would be boring for the entire semester. I was planning how I would combat sleepiness and boredom in the class and becoming more anxious as the mundane lecture drew longer and longer. However, the professor switched after 30 minutes of lecture into the last few minutes of class getting to know each other, and immediately my perspective on the class was changed."[4] Notice how quickly the challenge of paying attention leads to imagining future learning experiences. Hannah wondered aloud how she might have viewed the class differently if the interaction had come sooner. Sage similarly highlighted how the beginning of a class could leave her anticipating future negative experiences: "I have experienced circumstances in high school where the teacher walked in the classroom and told us to immediately grab our textbooks and get to work. The dynamic in the classroom following this bland introduction was lackluster and I would often dread having to spend an hour in the classroom with that teacher."[5]

Most striking to me were students' reflections on the consequences of ignoring the relational fabric of the group. Some commented that even when teachers invested time in learning the names of students, it was rare for time to be invested in students knowing anything about one another. That affected future interactions as courses progressed. Claire described being in a class in which she "never really got to know the other students." She noted: "It made for a tough transition when it came time to do randomly assigned group projects; we had no idea who was who or where to sit."[6] Maddy made a similar observation following our opening memory game. "We can work together if there are difficult assignments without feeling like strangers," she wrote. "I also felt like the professor cared about each person, instead of just seeing us as students to teach."[7] Aaron pointed to the connection between the opening activity and his sense of engagement: "The entire setup of the classroom made me realize . . . that the whole class is in this ride together, while in a typical classroom everyone sits down and doesn't talk on the first day. This makes me feel alone and it's just me in this classroom doing what I have to do to pass."[8] As we discussed the dynamics of collaborative work later in the semester, students returned to these themes, with many commenting that not knowing the students with whom they were asked to collaborate on group tasks made them more likely to just focus on getting the task completed with minimal interaction, resulting in something more like parallel solo effort than real collaboration. As FengYang expressed it, group work then becomes "more like individual work on a big assignment separately."[9]

I share these student responses neither because they are systematic data nor because this particular activity is now the correct way to begin class. I am simply seeking to illustrate how our opening moves in class are being read by students. Their first impressions can quickly turn into expectations about how the rest of the course is going to go. Those initial perceptions can change later; what happens next does of course matter a great deal. But they can also continue to influence future engagement.

I noted above that one of my goals was to model a way of teaching that was tethered to Christian concerns. I did not in this instance begin with devotions or prayer. If I had, then we would need to think about how the meaning of that beginning might depend on my posture, my tone, the topics mentioned in prayer, and the differing relationships to faith among my students. But on this occasion, I began without explicit religious behavior.[10]

Even so, my desire to lay the groundwork for building a community of mutual care in the classroom was informed by my faith. I was conscious that a course called "The Christian Teacher" had potential to generate anxiety, an expectation of official right answers backed by the might of Bible verses, or self-righteousness from instructor or students. I wanted to begin to build norms of interaction that could sustain us in humble, reflective, honest inquiry. I wanted to avoid looming over the students at the beginning. I also wanted to sow some seeds in preparation for reading theological accounts of Christian community two weeks later and discussing what they might have to do with teaching (see CONNECTING). None of this means that Christian doctrine authorizes my opening activity as the best way to proceed. It does mean that my choices were informed by my faith along with whatever wisdom I have gained about how learning works.

There are many valid ways to begin, yet there are also less optimal ways, not just in terms of whether they succeed at getting learning started but also in terms of what story they imply. Our first actions in a course can communicate courage or anxiety, hope or cynicism, isolated productivity or communal inquiry, delight in the world or the need to control, pride in our status or humility, the pursuit of shalom or consumer boredom, vulnerability to students or self-protection. Our first actions give hints to students about who we think they are and what they are likely to experience at our hands. Being intentional about how we start is one way of stating what we value.

Exercises

- Choose a course or sequence that you teach. What is the first thing that students are asked to do? Do they do it alone or together, aloud or in silence, quickly or slowly? What do those first moves imply about what will be important in the course? What do those opening moves suggest regarding your beliefs about teaching and learning?
- What do students learn in the first week of your classes about how they should expect to relate to one another during the semester? Make your own notes on this and then invite some of your students to share their own perceptions.
- Identify one Christian conviction that you hold about your students and their needs. Outline one way in which it could be communicated, explicitly or implicitly, through an opening activity in a course or topic sequence. Then set that activity aside and repeat the exercise, connecting the same conviction to a different opening activity. Enlist a friend or colleague in a conversation about the benefits and drawbacks of each activity.

CONNECTING

COMMUNION IN GIFTS AND GRACES

Christianity has specific things to say about how human beings are meant to relate to one another. One thing that all teachers do, intentionally or unintentionally, is help shape connections and interactions among the participants in a class or a school, whether in an elementary school classroom or a graduate seminar. The way we connect with one another during teaching and learning is therefore a fertile place to focus attention if we want to think about how "Christian" and "teaching" might go together.

Soon after I began teaching at a Christian university, I asked a student to help me return a pile of quizzes. She passed out several, then paused, apparently at an impasse. After a brief moment of indecision, she resorted to calling out names to identify the remaining recipients. I was a little taken aback. The class was not large, I had been calling on students by name every day, and it was now several weeks into the semester. Yet this student evidently did not know the names of many of the other class participants. I realized that I had just assumed that students would connect with one another over time as needed. I told students things. I told them to do things. I even told them to do things together. But I provided little that might help them learn to support one another's learning.

While relationships are an important focus in education for the youngest children, it is not obvious at all levels of teaching that fostering community or developing mutual responsibility should be a course goal. In *On Christian Teaching*, I mentioned a graduate seminar in which such goals were explicitly rejected. When a student suggested that the participants introduce themselves, the professor retorted that seminar participants were just "sources of argument," and so "it does not matter who you are or where you come from. What matters is the quality of your argument."[1] This might be unusually blunt, but I think it resonates with a wider unease that becomes more common as students get older. Elementary school classrooms commonly have a strong relational focus, yet as we move up through the education system, we are more likely to run into the sentiment that a classroom is not a social club. We assemble to focus on learning and the demands of the discipline, not to make friends. Despite the false dichotomies, there is a grain of truth in this worry. I can learn a lot in a class without paying much attention to those around me, and we might call the result successful learning. Time is tight. Might taking time to focus on community undermine goals more central to the teaching agenda?

Two convictions push me away from this conclusion. One is that academic learning and relational connection are not in fact competing goods, as if we could only pursue one goal at once. The two goals can be mutually supportive. As the COVID pandemic highlighted, social isolation does not optimize learning.[2] The other is that being Christian commits me to attending to the way we relate to each other in learning environments as in any other environment.

Christians have perennially reflected on the nature of community. This is not particularly surprising given the New Testament's emphasis on "one another" and the shaping of disparate people into a new body, a new temple, a new fellowship. This emphasis is sufficiently prominent that the major creeds and confessions in which churches across history have sought to summarize the essentials of their faith have commonly devoted space to the matter. Here is just one example, drawn from the Westminster Confession, a document produced by the 1646 Westminster Assembly to serve as a confessional framework for the Church of England:

> All saints that are united to Jesus Christ their head, by His Spirit and by faith, have fellowship with Him in His graces, sufferings, death, resurrection, and glory: and, being united to one another in love, they have communion in each other's gifts and graces, and are obliged to the performance of such duties, public and private, as do conduce to their mutual good, both in the inward and outward man. Saints, by profession, are bound to maintain an holy fellowship and communion in the worship of God, and in performing such other spiri-

> tual services as tend to their mutual edification; as also in relieving each other in outward things, according to their several abilities and necessities.[3]

I take it that Christian faith commits me to something like what is articulated here. There are other confessions and theological sources saying similar things, but there is plenty in this one to pause over and ponder.[4]

First, notice how our connectedness ("fellowship," "communion") is rooted in Christ, not in personal preferences. Our commitment to one another is not grounded in sharing the same politics, musical tastes, or ethnicity. It does not arise because we would have chosen the others to whom we are united or because they are our friends. It is grounded in God's prior choice to unite us in Christ, a choice not made based on our qualifications or identity markers. As Dietrich Bonhoeffer pointed out, if we confuse Christian community with our taste for the cozy feeling of being together with people we enjoy, we are likely to become disappointed with the actual people with whom we have been placed in fellowship. They will fall short of our dream of friction-free companionship, and before long we will become their accusers.[5]

Second, notice how grounding community in something other than our feelings of affinity leads directly to responsibilities and practices. We are "obliged" to the "performance of duties," and those duties are made up of whatever contributes to the "mutual good." The context includes "worship," but also "relieving each other in outward things," whether those things are "public or private." There is more at stake here than how we behave at church or whether we have the right inner attitudes. Our heart surely matters. So do our practices.

Community, according to this passage, means accepting that our connection to others is not grounded in our own likes and dislikes and embracing the consequent obligation to intentionally seek the good of others in all its facets and in every setting. While we are in a classroom together, our main goal is learning, yet that learning typically happens with others. The classroom is one of the public settings in which our calling to live in mutual service as a renewed humanity applies. The difficulty of the learning process and our various gifts and circumstances create a range of needs, anxieties, and struggles, inward and outward, that are opportunities for mutual care. Working to respond to those opportunities is part of our formation.

Cultivating Community

How can a classroom in which other students' learning is none of my business as long as I get the grade I need be a plausible outworking of "communion in one another's gifts and graces"? That was the question that weighed on me after realizing that students in my class did not necessarily even know one another's names.

The following semester, a student from that class asked me to mentor him. One day, sitting in the campus coffee shop, I referred back to the quiz distribution incident and lapsed into a minor rant. "I had not taught at a Christian college before coming here," I told him, "so I did not know exactly what to expect. But it sometimes feels as if each student is here to get their grade, and whether the person sitting two seats away succeeds or fails is none of their business. Other people are the teacher's job. And I am wondering how that can possibly be Christian. Am I my brother's keeper? What about 'love your neighbor as yourself'? Something feels wrong. I am wondering what I should be doing differently."

What stayed with me was the student's response. He was a deeply thoughtful individual with an articulate and passionate commitment to his faith. He had been through Christian elementary, middle, and secondary schools and had spent time at two prominent Christian universities. Yet the thought that discipleship might include taking some responsibility for the academic well-being of the people sitting around him in class struck him as an exciting new idea. He was animated with fresh possibilities. I wondered how he could get through that much Christian education and this be a new thought. Perhaps this was the moment when something other teachers had tried to tell him finally fell into place. Perhaps the fault lay with the deeply individualistic culture in which he had grown up. Or perhaps we should focus on the classroom cultures he had experienced in elementary, secondary, and higher education. Was the seating arranged in rows of individual, forward-facing chairs? Were assignments always designed to be done alone? Was collaboration construed as cheating? Was grading or the celebration of success always focused on individual performance? Did teachers talk for so much of the time that student interaction was minimal?[6] Did learning tasks ever focus explicitly on responsibility for others?

I can only speculate on the balance of influences in this particular student's formation. Yet thinking about the possibilities leaves me with questions for my own teaching. If the faith I profess commits me to a vision of "communion in each other's gifts and graces" and "relieving each other . . . according to [our] several abilities and necessities," what might that mean for the temporary pattern of interactions and mutual responsibilities shaped by the way I teach?

A teacher wrote to me from Tasmania about the kind of community she was building in her elementary school classroom. Her description illustrates how concrete and subversive a commitment to community can be. She has involved students in planning the wall displays and the layout of the classroom on the explicit basis of what will best serve everyone's needs. Describing the impact of this, she wrote:

> I remembered [hearing] about a teacher who was "done with show and tell" . . . and decided I was "done with the teacher desk." Now, my desk is a student desk, among the other student desks in the classroom. Often, an adult will walk in and ask, "Where is your teacher?" and I'm glad I'm not the focal point of the room anymore. When my students plan seating arrangements, they also plan for where I am positioned in the classroom. This has been an interesting experiment for everyone, and we are learning together about what works, what is kind, what is helpful, what communicates love and belonging. When I was working with one student as he completed a writing task, two students across from me were working on their seating plan for next term. I tuned in to their conversation. They were discussing friendships, work habits, academic needs, and how our diabetic student needs to be able to get to the office quickly without having to go past too many people because she gets embarrassed. A student nearby, looking over at their diagram, said, "Aaw, I want to be next to the teacher." One of the students working looked up and laid her hand on the student's arm. She said gently, "I think lots of people would. But Winter and Elijah need her more. Would you like to sit next to me or Vali? We will help you." I would like to point out that this mature response came out of the mouth of a seven-year-old. Last year, this

> student bullied others by exclusion, and found it difficult not to be the centre of my attention. Sometime between then and now she has been transformed, she has begun to grasp how to live in the growing community of faith and love we are cultivating in our classroom.[7]

I wonder whether my student, surprised by the idea that he was implicated in the academic well-being of others, experienced anything like this earlier in his education. I wonder how my own teaching was building on or amending what came before.

In a passage focused on the dynamics of Christian community, Paul tells us: "as we have opportunity, let us do good to all people, especially to those who belong to the family of believers" (Gal. 6:10). Love of neighbor is meant to govern our life in the wider world too, not just in church. Relationships with other believers are "especially" but not exclusively affected. If the vision of community articulated in the New Testament is an unveiling of how humanity should be, it should affect how I approach all kinds of relationships, especially when I have some responsibility for shaping how interactions happen. Choices as concrete as where to sit, how to arrange the furniture, how we interact, and who gets to speak reveal our sense of why others matter and shape students' experience of learning. When I teach, I get to make those choices, and in making them I bear witness.

Exercises

- Did your own experience of schooling lean more toward individual attainment or mutual responsibility? How has that influenced your own approach to teaching and learning?
- Read the paragraph quoted from the Westminster Confession again. Write the sentence stem: "if this is true, then when I am teaching I should . . ." Then complete the sentence at least five different ways with a focus on your own teaching setting. Then write five more sentences that begin: "My students might learn that this is true if . . ." Choose one sentence from your list and commit to acting on it in the next two weeks.
- Focus on a course or sequence you have taught more than once. Make two columns on a sheet of paper. In the first column, list the teaching

behaviors (arrangement of classroom resources, instructions, assignments, grading rubrics, etc.) that nudge students toward individual responsibility and self-reliance. In the second column, list those that nudge students toward mutual care and responsibility for one another. The two columns are not good and bad; both have value. What do you notice about their proportions and their relationship?

THE PERFORMANCE OF DUTIES

I turned to the Westminster Confession in the last chapter simply as one eloquent summary of some important strands of Christian reflection. If we trace the train of thought back to Scripture, we could dwell, for instance, on Paul's striking claim that in place of the identity boundaries of circumcision/uncircumcision, "the only thing that counts is faith expressing itself through love" (Gal. 5:6). In the wake of this, he goes on to draw a series of contrasts between the desires of the flesh and the desires of the Spirit. Although the language of "desires of the flesh" conjures up in modern imaginations a focus on bodily appetites, especially those connected to sex, that does not seem to be Paul's focus here.

The contrasts that Paul provides in Galatians 5 and 6 paint a cumulative picture of what belongs to "flesh" and what belongs to "Spirit." For instance, when he says "do not use your freedom as an opportunity to indulge your flesh, but through love serve one another" (5:13), the logic of the contrast suggests that "indulging the flesh" refers to behaviors that are the opposite of mutual service. When he warns us not to "bite and devour one another" and then counters that with "but I say, live by the Spirit and you will not carry out the desires of the flesh" (5:15, 16), he associates mutual hostility with the desires of the flesh. Such contrasts heap up throughout this section of Galatians, and in them the "flesh" is most frequently associated with discord and the Spirit with mutual care. John Barclay notes in a helpful and detailed discussion of this passage that the focus on love in this part of Galatians is not merely an ethics section appended to the real theology. It is the necessary, concrete expression of the gift of Christ worked out in the "creation and development of communities governed by new values and norms."[1] Elsewhere, Paul uses the image of parts of a body working in concert to evoke a kind of community in which "its parts should have equal concern for each other" (1 Cor. 12:22), a statement at once simple, eloquent, and radical. In such passages, we are asked not just to have new beliefs and values but to act differently.

In an earlier chapter (pp. 27–32), I offered some examples from syllabi of ways of framing course goals that focused on learning to treat one another well. Naming themes of mutual responsibility in my syllabus creates responsibilities for me as much as for my students. If Christian convictions about community entail an obligation to actively seek the good of others, and that obligation is to shape my teaching, I need to find teaching practices that could be described as faith expressing itself through love. Talking about community is a start; practices must follow.

The Gift of Practices

Intentional practices are not the same as techniques guaranteeing outcomes. Students are not programmable automata, and I cannot make Christian transformation happen through efficient technique. Writing of Christian practices more generally, Craig Dykstra suggests that "practices and disciplines are . . . gifts to the community, by means of which God may use the community to establish and sustain all people in the new life given by the Spirit."[2] Our practices do not command grace, yet grace may work through our practices.

I cannot force community, but I can lead my students toward working at it. I can create opportunities for us to test ourselves against an ethic of mutual service. We may fall far short in the implementation, and that falling short may itself be a key part of the learning. We might also find ourselves growing; there is evidence that well-structured, reflective assignments that ask students to interact with others outside class can help them to engage with people with whom they did not expect to have things in common.[3]

One practice with which I have been experimenting for several years involves assigned accountability groups. At the beginning of a semester, I often ask students to post short paragraphs of self-introduction on the class discussion board. I always meet students one-on-one to learn a little about them and find out their learning goals and needs. Both avenues can give me useful clues about how students in my class might cluster based on similar learning priorities and subject specialisms. I use what I learn to assign students to small accountability groups that remain stable throughout the semester. I usually wait until a week or two into the semester to do this, to give the intensity of the first week or so a chance to subside. This also lets me observe students a little before assigning groups. I want combinations that might lead to supportive dialogue, but I aim not to base the groups on friendship patterns. The kind of community that I have in mind is not primarily about personal affinity.

Each group ideally has four members, with adjustments for real-world class size. I give time early in the course to talking about the ground rules. The three other members of your group, I tell students, are the three class members for whose well-being you will take on a little more responsibility. That responsibility is not intended to involve heroic levels of commitment or crushing burdens. It involves small, manageable, concrete acts of care. These are likely to look different for students of different ages. I suggest a few examples that might work in my students' setting. For instance, if one group member is absent, others should notice and connect with them to find out why they are not here. You should help them secure a good set of notes, welcome them back to class when they return, and alert me if my help is needed. If one of them begins to struggle academically, you might offer to meet over coffee to go back over some recent material, or encourage them to connect with student support services and check in with me. If one of them is not clear about what this week's homework requires, you should be on their short list of folk they can easily ask, and you should ask them when you are the one with questions. As the semester wears on, and some of us become tired and discouraged, you should take the initiative with a timely note of encouragement or a supportive word. If I ask you to work together collaboratively as a group, part of your focus should be on how you can help deepen the learning of other group members and contribute to shared success. Whatever other needs and opportunities may arise, all that is expected and encouraged is an intentional focus on small, achievable acts of mutual support and respect. I will provide reminders and chances to take stock and recommit.

Students will get to interact with others outside their small group as we learn. It's just hard to care well for everyone in a large group, and the relative anonymity that can happen in a larger group can work against caring engagement. We only have so much time and attention, and we can always hope that someone else is taking care of things. The smaller group is intended to provide a practical focus. Each of us needs at least a small group of people who do not just regard us with broadly benevolent attitudes but actively see us and look out for us. I suggest to students that in ways appropriate to the temporary nature of our class and the pressures of our schedules, we can work to provide that for one another. We will fall short, but we can support one another in that too, offering to others the grace that we too will need. This is a chance to push beyond our tendency to look out for those we like, a chance to experience a little communion in one another's gifts and graces.

When I introduce this, there is an obvious risk that it will amount to little more than exhortation followed by increased guilt when life becomes too busy to keep track of one more thing. The pressures on all of us to stay in our furrows are real. The exhortation is more likely to be of benefit if supported by a regular rhythm of practice. The next step, then, is to look at how learning will be structured.

A simple step is to periodically have the groups sit together in class and allow them a few minutes to check in with each other and ask about each member's personal and academic well-being. At least once every other week, I also provide a task they are to do collaboratively with other group members.

I try to avoid the kind of group project in which a lot of individual work is followed by a few minutes of frantic coordination at the end, or in which one person does most of the compiling. I once overheard a group of students outside my office door discussing strategy for a group presentation in another class. Within two minutes they negotiated their way from "let's find some times we could meet" to "let's just meet once online" to "let's not meet, just email each of your bits, I'll put them together, and we can finalize the running order five minutes before class." Such tasks often result in little real connection, more often yielding frustration when a group member drops the ball. Having four names on a product does not guarantee that students learned much from or contributed much to one another.

I look for tasks where the focus is more on the process than on the product. After a reading or video, students might negotiate a prioritized list of key conclusions and questions in their group before whole class discussion. There could be different source material for each group member to study before class as preparation for teaching their part of the material to the rest of their group in class.[4] Many of these collaborations happen in class. If the task involves homework, I keep the time that students would need to meet outside class to a minimum, allow for the interaction to happen online, and supplement with time in class. Many students have demanding schedules, and not all live on campus.[5] Interspersing tasks in different group configurations allows for fresh input and a break from the same group dynamics.

The accountability groups do not usher in sudden wholesale transformation. They do give rise to a steady trickle of reports from students that they discovered small but significant ways in which connecting with others as they learn can bear fruit. In classes that involve a more substantial collaborative project later in the semester, these interactions lay important groundwork; students begin the more complex task with experience of working together on smaller pieces. The point here is not to find the single task that will fix things, but to construct a trajectory of practice across time that insistently nudges us toward attending to one another. This will look different in practical terms for a five-year-old and a graduate student, but each in their own fashion remains subject to the call to mutual service.

As I reflect on this a week before embarking on it afresh in a new semester, I am challenged again to keep an eye on my own focus. Sometimes my focus is more on my own efforts at consistency. If I believe that my faith commits me to a belief in community built on mutual service, then I should be looking for ways to bear witness to that conviction in my teaching practices. Sometimes my focus is more on student learning. I teach at a Christian university, and if students are to engage in learning that advertises itself as Christian, they should be helped to trace the threads between stated beliefs and the learning practices they experience, and they should have opportunities to engage in ways that might support their own spiritual growth. Both trains of thought seem relevant. Both risk leaving me standing by the roadside, pointing to the way rather than walking it. As I consider how my students might grow and how my class should be structured, I also need to avoid becoming the one who imposes community expectations without really being subject to them. I too will need to approach the other humans in my course and in my school as those whom I can serve and from whose gifts I can learn.

Exercises

- Read slowly though Galatians 5:1 to 6:10. Find every place where Paul makes a contrast: not this . . . but that; do not do this . . . rather that; if this . . . then not that. Use these to build up a picture, step by step, of what belongs to "flesh" and what belongs to "Spirit." Think about how either list is reflected in the dynamics of your classroom, and which triggers nudge those dynamics in one direction or the other.
- Look back and trace the steps of reasoning that lead from the Westminster Confession in the last chapter to the learning practices described in this chapter. Are the inferences valid? How might they apply to the age level at which you teach? If you set aside the sample strategy described in this chapter, in what other ways could you weave an emphasis on mutual service into teaching and learning?
- Find two or three colleagues who are interested in meeting to discuss teaching. Meet once a month for at least three months. Meet for an hour each time in a congenial setting away from the classroom, such as a coffee shop or outdoor space. Discipline your conversation to avoid complaints about students or circumstances. Focus on sharing:
    - the most fruitful teaching move you made in the last month, and what made it seem fruitful;
    - the least fruitful teaching move you made in the last month, and what you could do differently; and
    - one thing you would like to try to change in the next month.

  Commit to supporting one another's flourishing and focus the conversation on helping one another to grow. Offer encouragement as the opportunity arises between the meetings. Pray for one another's classroom.

LEARNING COMMUNITY PRACTICES

It is easy to imagine a concern for community as a kind of supportive relational backdrop to teaching content knowledge. We might focus on how we treat one another as a kind of parallel concern alongside the main business of learning. Perhaps it makes us kinder as we work yet remains incidental to what we teach and in the end dispensable when push comes to shove. But what if the relational fabric of the classroom is more intimately connected to questions about what it means to teach a subject area?[1]

A team at Calvin University comprised of a biochemist, a biologist, and a psychologist have been exploring just that kind of question. Rachael Baker, Amy Wilstermann, and Julie Yonker have been examining the connections between Christian practices for building and sustaining community, the demands of scientific collaboration, and the way we teach science classes.[2] Their work challenges the idea that focusing on how we relate to each other is a separate matter from getting a good science education, and their findings are suggestive for teaching other disciplines and at other age levels.

The lone genius ensconced in a warren of arcane equipment may be a recurring movie trope, but science is not typically done alone. Many of the most pressing problems that call for scientific solutions cannot be adequately tackled within the bounds of a single scientific discipline. Scientists collaborate extensively, and capacity for collaboration is important for scientific careers.[3] That capacity involves more than disciplinary expertise. Scientists may find themselves working in teams alongside others who have different identities, disciplinary tools and concepts, knowledge bases, and human failings. If scientific collaboration involves "social processes in which researchers pool their experience, knowledge, and social skills with the objective of producing new knowledge," then the way we relate to other humans in social settings is an important part of doing science.[4] The Science of Team Science investigates how such collaboration flourishes or flounders, and there are implications for how we approach teaching science.[5] Wilstermann notes that "equipping students with an understanding of the collaborative nature of science helps them to recognize and value the individual contributions of team members who bring a variety of skill sets, insights, and experiences to their work."[6]

Baker and Wilstermann decided to explore connections between the study of team science and the practices of intentional Christian communities. Through interviews with community members and site visits, they identified a range of broad practices that seemed to play a constructive role in enabling such communities to function. Those practices included hospitality, humility, learning together, self-reflection, gratitude, silence, and rest. The decision to focus on the practices that sustain community helped them to bridge to their own teaching context. Once we identify humility, for instance, not just as an inward attitude or value but also as a practice that helps sustain a community and enable its work, interesting avenues open up for making connections to teaching practices. If we turn to science classrooms, we can do so not just with the idea of exhorting students to be humble but with an interest in how practices that help develop and sustain humility can be encouraged while learning science.

Once relevant practices were identified, Baker and Wilstermann developed a classroom process for each practice that began with discussion of what the practice means, then offered opportunities for students to experience it, and finally followed up with some debriefing. In their words, it is important to "share why a practice is important, then take time to live it together before discussing the effect of the practice on learning, teamwork, and belonging."[7] Attending to each of these stages increases the likelihood that talk of gratitude or hospitality might move from functioning as nebulous ideals toward becoming conscious practices that can be learned, understood, and pursued. As Baker puts it, "we need a thriving community in our classroom, and for that we need to teach students how to build and participate in a thriving community."[8]

For Instance, Humility

Julie Yonker, the psychologist who helped evaluate the project, describes the steps involved in the team's approach to the practice of humility in the science classroom. The process begins with discussion of what we might mean by humility and what behaviors might be related to it.[9] Those behaviors include asking for help instead of pretending competence, listening to others with the expectation of learning from them, and being honest and realistic about one's capacities. In a Christian classroom, the context for such behaviors includes awareness of our creaturely dependence on God and lack of self-sufficiency and our call to exercise charity toward others.

Once shared understanding is established, students are asked to select a small intentional practice from a number of alternatives and focus on pursuing it for a week. For instance:

- At least once a week during class (either as part of the whole class or during a small group discussion), ask a question to the professor/teacher or a peer about something you don't understand.
- Admit when you do not know something, do not understand something, or do not know how to do something (do not pretend to have knowledge or abilities that you lack).
- Admit mistakes when they occur, rather than hide/ignore them.
- Ask for help when you need it.
- Display patience when others ask for help, or admit they do not understand something, or tell you that they have made a mistake, recognizing that these acts require humility (and courage).[10]

After a week of focusing on the chosen practice, students were invited to reflect on and discuss their experience and the effects on their learning, using questions such as these:

- Was this practice comfortable or uncomfortable for you? How did it change your experience in the classroom/lab?
- Why is humility important in community?
- Is humility a virtue that is valuable in leaders?
- Are there limits to the value of admitting mistakes, acknowledging lack of knowledge?

- Does humility have a place in competitive settings? If so, what does humility look like in an environment where prestige and recognition matter?[11]

Preliminary data gathered from students suggest gains in intellectual humility as well as gains in regular science learning.[12] Written student reflections convey their own perceptions of growth. "When looking back at my experience in the classroom, humility changed my orientation from me-focused to group-focused," wrote one. Another reported: "I also noticed that I was a happier person while intentionally practicing humility. The prideful mentality is a heavy load to carry while being a college student."[13] A third noted, "Being humble has elevated my learning experience because now, I get the chance to hear other people's thoughts and ideas as well as how they have come to their conclusion."[14]

Such student comments hint at how intentional relational practices might enhance rather than compete with the narrower task of learning science. As Yonker notes, "a classroom of humble individuals also creates efficiencies in how a classroom or team functions, namely, students are more willing to ask questions and be vulnerable in their learning, which makes it easier for the teacher to address areas of confusion, thereby saving time."[15] Pursuing the goods of mutually supportive community enhanced the ability to work well with others, listen well to others, communicate clearly and honestly, and request and receive input from their collaborators. These are learning goals that we can relate both to students' science learning and to spiritual and moral formation in community. In this case at least, the common instinct that sees investment in formational goals or intentional community as time stolen from covering the course material seems to be a misperception. A faith-informed hope for something more than test results need not compete with getting things done. Seeking "communion in one another's gifts and graces" is not a rival to the task of learning science, but rather a way of framing and pursuing that learning. It is a mode of learning science that can have connections to and benefits for real-world scientific practice.

Beliefs and Practices

Keeping the bigger theological frame in view matters for how we understand these teaching practices. We can turn just about anything, prayer and worship included, into a routinely managed substitute for genuine hope and dependence on grace. If we let a classroom emphasis on virtues such as humility or hospitality function merely as a set of instrumental techniques for improving the efficiency of science instruction, we begin to undermine the very commitments from which the process started. The purpose of Christian community is not to make lab work go better, even if lab work might go better in Christian community. This is one reason why the discussions with students before and after their practice experiments matter. What students and teachers imagine they are doing is part of what it will mean for them. It matters whether we are seeking to be changed in the light of grace or just looking for efficiency gains. It matters what kind of hope frames the practices.

While the project developed by Baker, Wilstermann, and Yonker focuses specifically on the science classroom and the collaborative processes involved in lab work, relatively little of it applies exclusively to the science curriculum. It is not difficult, for instance, to imagine similar processes and practices adapted to interpreting a literary work together. When I have asked students in literature classes to read one another's interpretations of a text, I have found them expressing surprise that others had seen such different things, despite having been in class discussions with those same students, and the exercise has led into discussion of why we might need one another in order to understand a significant text. How might a similar focus inform investigating a historical topic, or writing computer code? How might it work with younger students?

Whatever the specific disciplinary focus or age level, how we structure our interactions as we learn implies a vision of who we think we should become. This happens whether we focus our learning culture on competition, or mutual indifference, or passive listening, or the practices of intentional community. Teaching is intimately connected to how we think the connections and interactions among us should function. That question quickly pushes us back onto our beliefs about what it means to be a good human. We can choose to keep this kind of question out of sight, pretending that we are just covering material, or we can take responsibility for it and make it an intentional focus. We can let community be a vague ideal, or we can invest in specific practices that place our ability to live well with those around us in the light. Whichever way we choose, our underlying beliefs will be on display.

Exercises

- Before reading this chapter, would it have occurred to you to think of scientific laboratory work and the rhythms of intentional Christian community as connected in some way? Why/why not? What does your answer imply about the way you have learned to imagine learning?
- Summarize in your own words the difference between thinking of humility, hospitality, or gratitude as *attitudes* and thinking of them as *practices*. How might each emphasis affect how you connect them to teaching? Which emphasis better describes how you relate them to your own teaching?
- Choose one of the community-supporting practices listed by the team science project leaders: hospitality, humility, learning together, self-reflection, gratitude, silence, and rest. Choose a class that you teach. Identify three small, intentional practices that you could make an explicit part of learning and that would connect well to the content focus of your class. Make notes on how you would frame them for students and how you could give students chances to work on them for a specific time period and debrief. Share your outline with a colleague before trying it out, and report back to them afterward on what happened.

COMMUNITY BEYOND THE CLASSROOM

Some years ago, I had breakfast with some of my daughter's teachers.[1] We enjoyed a freewheeling conversation, imagining how school might be different. At one point we began to talk about homework, and I shared some of my sense of dissatisfaction with the status quo from my standpoint as a parent. My worry was this: during those teenage years when a strong and articulate relationship with our children seemed more important than ever, homework often seemed to reinforce isolation and separation. My daughter rose early to take a bus to school, spent a long day in school, and then rested for a while when she eventually returned home. We would eat an evening meal together. Often all of us were tired from our day, and it was not always our most articulate time. After the evening meal came homework, often in generous amounts so that completing it filled the bulk of the evening hours. What had particularly struck me was that the homework tasks always seemed to be designed to be done alone. The basic genres were read something, solve something, write something, or research something. Typically, the tasks drew our daughter to her room with a laptop and a pile of books.

The school's theology viewed parents as carrying primary responsibility for their children, and educators as partnering with and supporting them. Yet the most common roles available to me as a parent in relation to learning tasks were supervision ("have you started your project yet?") and occasional subversion ("it's late, you need to stop trying to make it better and get some sleep"). Neither role really felt as if it nurtured the fabric of our relationship with our daughter. This was what I was complaining about over breakfast: my sense that one of the negative pressures on how well we interacted with our daughter was the pattern of assignments at her Christian school, assignments that colonized the evening as well as the day and fostered solitude.

Over the following weeks, curious things started happening in our household. It started one evening when our daughter appeared in the living room earlier than usual, looking a little hesitant. She wanted to know if we had time to talk. She had an odd homework task from her religion teacher. She was supposed to ask us whether we grew up Christian or experienced a conversion, and how we thought our childhood had influenced who we had become. What she learned from the conversation would be the basis for class discussion, and we were to sign a slip confirming that the conversation had happened. A few days later she asked for another evening conversation. She had been assigned by a different teacher to find out what we thought about the government using drones for surveillance and warfare, a topic that had been in the news. The following week, she had to give a presentation in a media class with slides, and she informed us that she had to first give the presentation to us twice, soliciting feedback to help her improve it before she finally gave it in school. After each of these exchanges, we signed a slip to attest to our engagement with her learning.

None of the tasks required us to be expert in the subject area being taught. They merely asked for a little time, an opinion, and a willingness to have a serious conversation. All of the tasks involved us in meaningful interaction, allowed us to contribute to our daughter's learning, and balanced the isolation appropriate to other homework tasks with some relational engagement. We had (and have) a good relationship with our daughter, yet each of these times was a gift. Our daughter's verdict was that these tasks were more rewarding than the usual fare, and that she felt she learned more. Ours was that we had been gifted with rewarding conversations that we might have missed if teachers had not prompted them.

Hurdles to Negotiate

There are, of course, logistics involved in the background of such an enterprise. I would rather not have all of my daughter's teachers assign this kind of task on the same evening, so some communication among colleagues about scheduling is required. In our case, overload was happily avoided. Some students may not have access, or may not have quick access, to a parent or other adult willing to engage. A realistic timescale for completing the task, sensitive communication, and provision of alternatives, such as opportunities for conversations with teachers or other safe community members, are important for those students.[2] In a higher education setting like the one where I work, parents may not be accessible, but other possibilities multiply with a campus full of adults in a range of roles. Given a sufficient window of time, I can quite realistically ask my students to find out someone else's perspective on an issue, teach something to a peer, or practice summarizing a reading to another person. Of course, if we assign tasks requiring interaction, the tasks themselves need to be meaningful and capable of sustaining good conversation and inquiry, not just one more variety of busywork for all involved. Filling out worksheets together or answering yes/no questions might not have been quite as rewarding for us or our daughter.

Success may not be instant or universal. In my own first year in teaching I began to experiment along these lines with homework tasks. When I taught beginner-level French to eleven-year-olds, I asked them after the first week to take home a certificate that said "Thanks to [space for name of student] I can now, in French, introduce myself and say where I live. Signed [space for name of parent]." The student was to teach their parent the French phrases they had been learning and bring the certificate back as proof. I wanted to give my students a sense of achievement based on the awareness that they had already learned to do something that many of the adults in their lives could not do.[3] I also wanted to strengthen family interaction and provide a little shared fun.

Mostly it went well. Yet one student returned and awkwardly took me aside. "Me mum told me to git lost and not be so stupid," he confessed. The episode taught me about the need to provide options and communicate well ahead of time with parents, but if anything, it strengthened my resolve to see if I could design tasks that helped students build connections with their adult social world. Lack of guaranteed compliance does not necessarily make something a bad idea. Dysfunction in my students' relationships with the adults in their lives was part of the world not being the way it was supposed to be, and therefore something to resist, not a parameter to which I should simply submit.[4]

As I talked more with the teachers who had shared the initial breakfast conversation, I learned that in their case, too, not every parent had been immediately thrilled, though some of the frictions were in the end not a bad thing. One assigned a homework task that invited students to choose and watch a TV show with their parents and then discuss with them its implicit value system. One set of parents contacted the teacher the following week. They had been unable to find a long enough time segment during the week when they were all in the same place. They realized that something was wrong and resolved to find ways of spending more time together as a family. Some years later, I led training at another area school that included discussion of the possibilities for this kind of homework. A few days after the training, I received an email from a stranger who was the parent of a child at the school. They wrote that they were not sure exactly what I had done with the teachers at the training day, but it was already positively affecting the dynamics of their family life.

Not every kind of friction is bad news. If the friction pushes us up against good questions about how we can live well together, perhaps we should welcome it. Despite the real obstacles to be considered, my sense is that teachers have more cultural power in this area than they think they do. Teachers are among the few people in society who can tell others what to do with their free time and more often than not be obeyed. I spent hours driving around town helping my children to collect leaves because a teacher assigned a leaf project. That teacher's task choice shaped my entire weekend. The power to direct how others use their time is a significant responsibility. How constructively do we use it?

When we think about how faith connects with education, it's easier to focus on the big ideas that we teach, or the character traits that we model in class, or whether we relate to students in a caring way. The default practices that make up the supporting routine easily pass unchallenged. They are just part of how we do school, and our mind's eye slips past them to the content we want to insert into the schooling receptacle. Homework, like testing, grading, and talking from the front, is one of those default practices that seem to come automatically with the package of schooling. We think we know what homework must look like because it has been done to us. When the default patterns end up scripting what we do, we spend more time finding things to fill the next homework slot than wondering what homework is and what kind of learning we should hope it will achieve.

The tasks that we assign outside class are one more way of communicating what we value. They reveal what we assume about our students and their needs. They reveal how we think learning fits into students' lives. They reveal how we think the world should be known. If the faith that we bring to the learning process includes a hope for communion in one another's gifts and graces, a belief in the good of mutual service, and an awareness that we need to grow through practice in our capacity for seeking the mutual good, then perhaps we should question how many of the learning tasks that we create have to be designed to be done alone.

Exercises

- The last sentence of this chapter refers back to phrases from the chapter "Communion in Gifts and Graces" (pp. 47–53). How did we get from the Westminster Confession and its theology of community to the practicalities of assigning homework? Take a moment to retrace the connecting moves. How might homework be reshaped in a similar manner by other basic commitments, for instance, by a commitment to seeking justice, or walking humbly, or loving mercy?
- How often in the average semester are your students assigned homework activities
    - that require meaningful interaction with the adults in their lives around questions of meaning and purpose?
    - that draw them into collaborative learning and focus explicitly on the skills and dispositions needed to learn with and from others?
    - that give them firsthand insight into the lives of other people in their community, especially those they might normally ignore?
    - that involve them in active service and justice seeking together with others?
- Design one homework activity that you could use with your students that will bring them into constructive dialogue with (other) adults and contribute to the richness of their relationships outside the classroom. Include a plan for communicating with affected adults and for making provision for students whose circumstances create barriers to carrying out the task.

FRAMING

SPEAKING, HEARING, HOSPITALITY

Teachers do not simply list course content for learners. They sequence it in ways that imply a story about what fits together and where it is headed. They include visuals that activate some associations and discourage others. They leave some things unmentioned, creating eloquent absences. They name material in ways that imply an angle from which it can be viewed. Teachers frame learning for learners—they cannot do otherwise—and in doing so they imply a story about what learning means.

Speaking and Hearing

One day more than a decade ago, I received an unexpected phone call in my campus office.[1] It turned out to be a former student. Matt had been in my second-year German courses, part of his language requirement. It quickly emerged that he was now calling from Germany and had a story he was bursting to tell.

His morning had involved a bus journey. The bus was quite full, and as it picked up more passengers a young German man took the vacant seat beside him. He seemed visibly dejected. Matt recalled learning in class that striking up conversations with strangers in public was less common in German culture than back in the United States, but he figured that as a foreigner he could maybe get away with it. He asked the man how he was. The man's story spilled out. He was on his way home from his workplace, where he had just been fired. He was going to have to tell his wife that he had lost his job. He was not sure what he would say.

"Then I remembered what you said in class!" Matt exclaimed.

My first reaction was a moment of anxiety. What had I said in class? What unscripted moment was coming back to haunt me now?

Matt reminded me of a day in class when I had displayed the German text of Deuteronomy 6:4, "Höre, Israel, der HERR, unser Gott, ist ein einiger HERR."[2] (Hear, O Israel: the Lord our God, the Lord is one.) I had been reading a commentary by Walter Brueggemann in which he reflected on the relationship between listening, self-will, and vulnerability.[3] As long as I am listening, I am vulnerable. I am waiting on words that I do not yet know, words that could hurt or heal, affirm or reject, inspire or unsettle. "The alternative to listening is autonomy," Brueggemann suggests, a state of self-sufficiency in which I choose my own way.[4] I can maintain my own sense of control more easily when I am the one speaking. In Jeremiah, God's repeated complaint against Israel was that they failed to listen. The Israelites were called to listen before they were called to speak: "Hear, O Israel." Yet instead of hearing well, "Israel organized its life for self-serving and self-sufficiency."[5] As far as Jeremiah was concerned, the way the Israelites attended to their neighbor and their ability to listen were deeply interconnected: "You must treat one another fairly. Stop oppressing resident foreigners who live in your land, children who have lost their fathers, and women who have lost their husbands. . . . You also have done all these things, says the Lord, and I have spoken to you over and over again. But you have not listened!"[6]

Neither the commentary nor the biblical passages were about language teaching, but I prepared for class that day with this contrast between listening and self-absorption rolling around in my mind. After commenting briefly on how the Deuteronomy text emphasized listening, I asked my students whether it had ever struck them that we always talk about speaking other languages. We claim to be able to speak German. We ask people if they can speak Chinese. It is much less common to ask people if they can hear Russian, if they are able to listen to speakers of Spanish. What might that say about how we imagine our relationship to our neighbor, about our capacity for hospitality to others? It seems as if we imagine the languages of others mostly as additional channels through which we might be able to assert our own agendas, broadcast our own thoughts, and meet our own needs. We think of language learning as an enhancement of our own agency, which it is. We less often ask which fresh voices a new language might allow us to hear. Does the way we talk about learning the languages of others make the process more about us than about our neighbor?

These were the comments that Matt now called back to my mind as he spoke to me from Germany. As the bus passenger next to him shared his story, Matt remembered me saying that we are not just learning German so that we can speak to Germans more, but so that we can listen, so that we can be hospitable to our neighbor. So he sat and listened as the young man unfolded his story. "At the end, he thanked me for listening to him and giving him a chance to talk through what happened before he talked to his family," Matt concluded. "I had to call you and tell you what happened!"

I still think back to this conversation with a kind of wonder. If a past student calls me from overseas, and what animates him is not that he saw a major tourist site, but that he got to listen to an unemployed person on a bus, then something a little mysterious has just happened. Of course, it is also not very repeatable. The lesson here is not that if we quote Deuteronomy in class, we should expect that our students will counsel folk in crisis on foreign buses. Matt's response was personal, and his circumstances were unusual.[7]

Yet I do think this sequence of events has some wider relevance. When I foregrounded speaking and listening and connected the distinction to theology and ethics, I offered my students a fresh way of framing what they were doing. Frames matter for how we perceive things. Imagine a famous painting in a cheap clip frame, or a postcard in a gilt frame, or the *Mona Lisa* in a frame with a tiny aperture that only lets us see her left eyebrow. When we teach course content, the way we name it, the facets we hide or make visible, the connections we make or fail to make all serve as frames, inviting our students to relate to the content in particular ways. My German students do not just learn German. They learn whether learning German is connected to faith, ethics, and service, or just to shopping, travel, and getting into grad school.

Since that phone call, I have often wondered (and sometimes tried to find out) exactly what students think we are doing when we learn together in class. Yes, we are, for instance, learning German. But are we, at the back of our mind, just checking off requirements, or doing what we are asked without asking why, or learning to serve our neighbor, or enhancing a future travel experience, or enhancing our employability, or practicing hospitality, or . . . ? How students imagine learning is affected by their own varied experiences and priorities, but also by the frame I provide, the story I tell about learning. Different stories position us differently, offering different ways of pointing ourselves at the world. It matters not only what we teach, but how we name it and what students imagine we are doing while we teach it.[8]

Civic Hospitality

Themes of hospitality and listening also loom large in the Civic Hospitality Project.[9] This recent curriculum project was rooted in the conviction that the familiar appeal to tolerance is insufficient as a frame for approaching the polarization and intergroup hostilities that seem rife in contemporary society. The call to tolerance asks me to put up with your differences in exchange for you being willing to put up with mine. A Christian frame asks for more, extending the idea of love of neighbor to include strangers, even enemies. What if our need, as those who must live with people who are different, is not just to tolerate them, but to learn a civic hospitality that does not make conformity a precondition for loving others as our neighbors?[10]

This frame shift quickly nudges us toward some pedagogical questions. If our need is the capacity to practice hospitality even when it is tempting to substitute indifference or hostility, then we need more than information or discussion. We need ways of working on the skills and attitudes that can sustain hospitality as a practice. If we want students to internalize hospitable dispositions, then it does not seem plausible to rely on modes of teaching that focus on one-way communication or a set of correct answers. If we want students to think of hospitality in terms closer to Jesus's practice of welcome than to the displays of affluence and refined taste associated with hospitality by current lifestyle gurus, we will need ways of helping students to think theologically about the concept.[11] If we change the frame for the civics classroom from tolerance or civic competence to the pursuit of hospitality in public spaces, the common emphasis on knowledge about government structures and skills for participating in political processes soon feels too small.[12]

Kelli Boender, a team member in the Civic Hospitality Project, describes the experience of developing and teaching social studies classes framed by a call to civic hospitality at a Christian high school.[13] Students studied and discussed Jesus's practices around table fellowship and inclusion, and developed a shared class list of "daily hospitable acts" to which they held one another accountable. One class activity involved having students read news reports on a controversial issue in groups and then discuss their findings, only to discover when they compared findings that different groups had received different articles displaying different biases. They debriefed the experience together, analyzing their reading process and how they responded to encountering contrasting accounts of the same events. They related the whole process to ideas of hospitality and of others as made in God's image.[14] As the semester progressed, Boender reports, "I saw a shift in our class norms where students became uncomfortable with a one-sided narrative as they recognized that as inherently inhospitable."[15] She describes this fundamental reframing of her social studies teaching as challenging yet ultimately rewarding work:

> Placing hospitality at the forefront of your mind when planning lessons and designing curriculum is tiring. I can attest to that after this school year. But this was a different kind of tiredness than the way I have felt before as I engaged in politically charged or conflict-ridden topics. Hospitality made conflict exhausting but also fulfilling. I found my faith restored and strengthened over this past year of teaching as I saw the work in our project bear fruit with my students. I felt confident addressing conflicts with parents about curriculum or class content and I even had parents reach out to me and say thank you for bringing ideas to their own dinner tables.[16]

As with the idea that language study is about learning to hear others, the process here started with an intentional act of naming. Civics education was framed by a Christian understanding of hospitality.

Such acts of naming can, of course, be glib and superficial, a quick Christian gesture before we return to business as usual with little really changed. They can be moralizing moves that tell students to be good people but fail to connect with the whole of their learning or to model what is urged. They can be moments of oddity, offering a frame that is not well grounded and that sits at best awkwardly with the course content. In such cases little of worth will be achieved by changing our words.

Yet they can also be ways of helping us to see differently what we are doing and so to begin to do it differently. The process Boender describes is one where the teacher takes the act of renaming seriously enough to invest in the way of being for which it calls and works it into the fabric of classroom practices. That kind of reframing has the potential to become transformative. It is more than a momentary shift of label or a pious aside. It becomes an embodied invitation to move together in a shared direction, sustained by a shared naming of the destination for which we are aiming. The teacher not only points the way but walks the road.

We cannot teach without offering some kind of frame. I wonder, what pictures do our words paint of what learning is about? What do our students think we are doing when we teach? What do they think they are doing when they learn? How exactly are we contributing to either facet of their imagination through the frames we offer?

Exercises

- Read Genesis 18:1–8, Isaiah 25:6–8, and Luke 14:1–24, preferably more than once and in conversation with others. Consider what each passage adds to an understanding of hospitality that could serve as a frame for learning the languages, cultures, and perspectives of others. How could these emphases influence an approach to teaching and to course content?
- Reflect and journal on the questions in the last paragraph of the chapter: How do you think your students imagine the teaching and learning processes in your classroom? Toward what ends do they think those processes are building? In how many ways do you contribute to their picture of what is happening? How could you find out whether your answers to these questions are accurate?
- Choose a topic or course that you teach and write down a considered answer to the question: How does learning this fit into living before the face of God? Then review how your answer to this question is reflected in how you communicate with students about why assigned tasks are important.

CODING AND BEAUTY

Talk of appealing to biblically resonant frames such as hospitality to strangers may work for those aspects of the curriculum focused on studying humans, but what about technical courses?[1] A class in computer programming, for instance, seems like a good candidate for a purely technical course. Computer code doesn't much care whether you are Christian when it runs; it works or it doesn't. The skills needed by learners seem clearly delineated. We can pause every now and then to ask bigger questions about the purpose and use of technology, but when we focus on learning how to code well, there seems less wiggle room for worldviews. Yet the way Victor Norman, one of my colleagues at Calvin University, approaches his courses in computer programming offers another window into the question of how we frame things for ourselves and for our learners.

Virtuous Coding

Norman invites his students to view their coding work through the lens of a range of virtues, including hospitality, humility, and honesty. He wants his students to "write good code . . . but with a different motivation."[2] He uses this frame to focus students on what is happening when they write code. His grading rubric includes credit, for instance, for writing hospitable code, an inclusion that triggers discussion with students about what that might mean. Asking for accurate code would raise few eyebrows, but hospitable code? Most of the code they write as computer programmers will be used by others. What happens to the way code is written if the programmer focuses on making the work of the next person in the chain easier and more fruitful? Active attention to the well-being of the colleague who will use or extend the code affects "the good variable names, the spacing, the comments, the clean code, and how we're trying to communicate this to others who are reading the code."[3]

Similar concerns emerge from talk of humility and honesty. Norman connects humility to the realization that after completion and testing, code still has limitations and will likely not function as well in every conceivable circumstance. Humility invites attention to what has not been achieved, rather than hasty closure. What unforeseen user behavior could crash the program? What inputs that did not occur to the programmer might make sense to some other user? Honesty calls for documenting, rather than ignoring, hiding, or glossing over, the limitations and liabilities of the code. As Norman points out, these are all concrete ways of loving one's neighbor in the specific context of coding work. "These three virtues," he comments, "are all about loving others, which is what God wants us to do, love others, not just create stuff but love others with what we create."[4]

This frame is not what students are typically expecting from an introduction to computer programming. "I think they're surprised by the virtues language," Norman reports. "It makes them wonder a little bit and think a little bit."[5] They are still learning the practical details of how to code, but the anticipated frame has shifted, and that opens the possibility of other kinds of learning (without sacrificing any basic coding competence). This way of framing the class offers a picture of the world in which technical activities do not happen in a realm disconnected from faith and ethics. It is a picture in which the work of the computer programmer is carried out in the presence of the neighbor and before the face of God. The shift of frame implies a claim about what the work is and a story about how students should grow if they are to become good at it.

Frames and Identities

We might at first imagine acts of framing as decorative, leaving the picture inside the frame untouched. Coding is still coding, and compiling code still works the same way. Once we notice that learning includes the learner's experience of learning, the picture changes. We can experience learning to code just as increasing prowess in a technical skill, or also as an act of care toward our neighbor. The contrast recalls Etienne Wenger's evocation of two stonecutters carving stone, one thinking that they are trying to cut the stone into precise shapes, the other thinking that they are helping to build a cathedral.[6] Their work may be indistinguishable if we consider only their precision with the chisel, yet they may be experiencing and learning different things as they work. As Wenger puts it, a particular "infrastructure of imagination" provides the context in which we develop an "identity of participation," a way of being ourselves that grows out of what we sense is expected of us in a specific community of practice.[7] Empirical research suggests that our thinking is highly sensitive to how ideas are framed. Changing a metaphor can influence our opinions to a degree that overrides our existing beliefs, and underlying metaphors may influence our decisions even when we are not conscious of the fact and justify our choices on other grounds.[8] How we frame things to ourselves and to others matters for what we experience ourselves as doing and who we become.

If frames have consequences, then we should approach them with care, lest they amount to deception, fantasy, or a harmful form of indoctrination. Is Victor Norman pulling the wool over his students' eyes, illegitimately hoodwinking them into thinking religious thoughts while they compose lines of code? Notice that he openly invites his students to discuss the proposed frame with him, to explore together whether ideas such as hospitality are really relevant to coding. The frame is not a hidden stratagem, but a part of what students are asked to think about in the course. This does not take away the fact that he is choosing which frame is discussed. But if we frame coding as a purely technical exercise, or a ticket to a more lucrative career, or progress toward an increasingly technological future, or a means to academic credit, these too are partial, chosen frames, not unadorned reality. Each also offers a story about what is happening that starts from somewhere. We cannot teach without some kind of frame. The best we can do is be responsible with the frames we offer.

A second question worth asking here is whether Norman's approach amounts to moralizing. Is the suggestion here that content learning needs a moral homily to accompany it? If we take any topic in the curriculum and add some virtue talk, is that what will make it Christian?

Not only in general terms, but also in Norman's specific case, I think that would be a hasty conclusion. In fact, there are signs in his description of his own work that more is afoot. To get at what it is, let's take a detour via a prayer about beauty.

Beauty

Norman asks his students "not just to get the grade but to create something beautiful, create something hospitable."[9] In an article about whether computer programming is a form of artistry, he explores various criteria for considering code beautiful: clarity, elegance, robustness, simplicity, and more.[10] He approaches these qualities not just as properties of the code but in the context of presenting code to those who need to use and rely on it. In this telling, the virtues framing how we present our creative work to others become part of a story about what is beautiful, a story that others have explored in courses in, for instance, biology and mathematics.[11]

The present book began with an image of a teacher and a student by the road to wisdom drawn from Comenius's *Orbis Pictus*. Comenius also wrote several significant treatises on education. The most famous, the *Didactica Magna* (Great Didactic), closes with a prayer for beauty composed from a collage of allusions to the Psalms: "God, strengthen what you have worked in us. (Ps. 68:29) May your work be evident to your servants, and your beauty be upon their children. Indeed, may the delightfulness of God our Lord attend us and may he align the works of our hands. (Ps. 90:16) I have trusted in you, Lord, may I never be brought to ruin."[12] Comenius closes his account of education by asking for God's beauty (*decor*) to be upon our children and for God's delightfulness (*amoenitas*) to attend us as God brings the works of our hands into their proper alignment. After all the toil of defining grade levels, subject divisions, and learning strategies, the final note is a call for delight, for beauty.

English translations of Psalm 90 vacillate over the word here rendered "delightfulness," some leaning more toward an emphasis on attractiveness (beauty, brightness, loveliness, delightfulness, pleasantness) and some favoring a focus on positive regard (favor, kindness, approval, blessings). John Goldingay's choice of "delights" perhaps captures something of both.[13] It seems that the beauty here is not just a beauty of form, but a beauty of gentle holiness, a beauty that is as close to kindness as to shining. This is a beauty in which the moral, the theological, and the interpersonal are not clearly distinguished because everything shines at once. It was this simultaneous shining that Comenius tried to capture earlier in his book when he insisted that careful thinking, growth in virtue, and delight in God must be thought of as inseparable if we are to have something worth calling education.[14] His closing prayer does not sound to me like a prayer for our teaching to merely be accurate or efficient, or for it to have a moral exhortation or a Bible verse added. It sounds like a prayer that our teaching in its complex fabric might somehow reflect something of the face God turns to the world.

That larger picture is, I think, what generates the instinct for Christian teachers to ask more limited questions such as what learning German has to do with hospitality or what coding has to do with honesty. What if we imagined such questions less as opportunities to insert a quick burst of moral instruction, and more as ways of wondering what it would be like for the beauty/favor/brightness/kindness of a compassionate/just/patient God to shine on and through our teaching and scholarship?

However we put the pieces together, the frame out of which we teach (consciously or unconsciously) helps direct students' attention to the kinds of learners we hope they will become, and it hints at the kind of world we think we live in. If we live in a divinely composed creation originally marked by a wholeness in which all things cohere, then the idea that beauty, kindness, and learning to create accurate, elegant strings of computer code belong together will not seem particularly strange. There will be times for concentrating hard on the details to be mastered. There should also be times for naming what the brushstrokes contribute to the picture.

Exercises

- How do you imagine the place of technical courses in the curriculum? Where does this imagination come from? Did this chapter unsettle it in any way?
- Choose a course or topic that you teach and find a way to ask students (e.g., through discussion, journaling, or a focus group) why they think they are learning it. Compare their answers to your own account of why you are teaching it, and then to the questions about

beauty raised in this chapter. Where is there overlap or tension among the three accounts?

- Return to the phrase "may your beauty be on their children," and to the discussion of beauty that follows it. How might the things you teach participate in that kind of beauty? How could you communicate this to students, not just through direct speech but through design of learning activities?

IMPLICIT STORIES

In the last two chapters I have focused on how we name what we are doing when we teach, but there are other kinds of framing. In an earlier chapter (pp. 33–38), I described different ways of starting a language course: an invitation to wisdom, a list of things and elements, and a focus on the self and its possessions and pleasures. Three books, three ways of framing language learning through an opening move: Are we primarily pilgrims, observers, or consumers? The beginning gives us clues about where we are headed, but the shape of the ensuing journey provides a further frame for learning. What sequence of topics and pattern of emphases might most fittingly unfold in the wake of each of those beginnings?

As before, I invite you to think back to your first experiences of learning a new language in school. Chances are, you had a textbook of some kind. Picture it. Imagine yourself opening the front cover. What topics would you find on the contents page? What themes would receive the most space? What would not be mentioned?

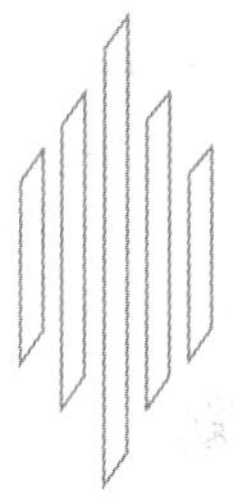

Into the Time Machine

Now let's rewind to the seventeenth century and the *Orbis Pictus*.[1] After the chapter on wisdom comes the chapter on God, where we are introduced to the members of the Trinity, "the chiefest Good, and the only inexhausted Fountain of all good things."[2] Next come the world and the heavens, the elements, clouds, and the earth. There follows a lengthy sequence of chapters each introducing a kind of creature found in the world: rocks, plants, fruits, insects, fish, birds, mammals, and so on. The order broadly echoes the Genesis account of creation.

In chapter 36, we finally come to human beings. Across several chapters we learn about the creation and fall of Adam and Eve, the stages of life, the parts of the male and female body, the senses, the soul, and those who "differ in the body from the ordinary shape."[3] Next, we survey a wide range of human callings and contexts, from gardening and making honey to mining and writing, among many others; there are over fifty chapters in this part of the book. Included among these is a sequence on food that begins with comment on the declining social status of agricultural workers; proceeds through various ways of gathering food; shows people making flour, baking, and cooking; and culminates in a chapter on the practice of hospitality at a shared meal. Chapter 98 talks about schools, followed by music, philosophy, geometry, and astronomy.

Chapter 109 begins a section on moral philosophy that includes chapters on prudence, diligence, temperance, courage, patience, kindness, justice, and generosity. Social relationships (marriage, employment, parenting) are then examined, followed by cities, justice, commerce, and recreation. A brief survey of the military and warfare is followed by a comparison of the major world religions.

Threaded through the preceding sections is recurrent attention to calamity and suffering. Tornadoes, shipwrecks, suicide, sieges, sea battles, and drowning are all given space. Finally, in the last two chapters, the story is brought to a close with discussion of God's providence and the final judgment.

Obviously this textbook is from the seventeenth century and contains topics and assumptions that are not of our time. My students have no pressing need for material on how to shoe horses, and talk of bodily variations as "monstrous" is best left in the past. Yet the text can still speak to us if we focus instead on what kinds of things are included and how they are sequenced. What comes first and last? (Wisdom/God and judgment.) What is given more space (nonhuman creatures, virtues, professions, suffering) or less space (travel, school, monetary transactions, personal preferences)? What is thought worth emphasizing and what is left out? As we move from creatures to people, callings, sufferings, virtues, society, faith, and final accountability, what kind of world is evoked?

Imagine yourself a student in a language class using this text, day after day for a year or two. It does not look weird to you; the other children in your class are using the same text. As far as you know, this is what language textbooks have looked like since the beginning of the world. Over time, you gain skills and knowledge; this was an enormously successful language textbook. What else do you learn? What assumptions do you imbibe about what it means to be a good student, to be a good person, to succeed at school? Who are the winners and the losers? For what kind of life do you imagine yourself preparing, and why?

A Leap Forward

Fast-forward to the eighteenth century and *The London Vocabulary*. We have already seen (p. 34) that it begins with things and elements. Many of the chapters on creatures from the *Orbis Pictus* are squashed into two lists of "things," ranging from crumbs to minutes, and from God to clay. From there we range over minerals, plants, trees, insects, birds, fish, and "beasts." Each gets a single short chapter consisting of an image and a list of names. The human mind and body are treated for a few chapters, again without narrative context. A chapter titled "Meats and Drinks" offers a list of foods, followed by chapters on clothes, buildings, and "household stuff."[4] After brief treatment of the countryside, with some farming vocabulary, a sequence on society includes a chapter each on the school, the church, the judiciary, and the military. After this there are no more pictures, and the closing chapters deal with time (just the basic divisions of time in hours, days, and seasons, not the larger arc of history) and various grammatical categories. The book ends with a brief chapter on "interjections," teaching us how to say "oh!" and "hush!" in Latin.[5] The text throughout appears in list form, a collection of things falling under various categories.

This book deals with far fewer topics than the *Orbis Pictus*. It is interesting to note what has been targeted for omission. Wisdom, the Fall, and the stages of life are gone. Women have disappeared from the chapter on body parts. The soul is replaced by "the Mind and its Affections."[6] Most forms of labor and service have disappeared. Most of the material on agriculture, food preparation, and hospitality is gone. Virtues, relationships, suffering, and comparative religion are all gone. Providence and the final judgment are gone, replaced at the end by grammatical categories.

Charles Taylor argues that the gradual change in our shared imagination that nurtured the secular societies of Western modernity involved several related changes in how we picture our place in reality.[7] We shifted from seeing the world as an ordered cosmos, in which each creature had its place and calling within God's design, to seeing the world as a universe: vast, mostly empty, and governed only by physical laws. At the same time, we changed how we imagine ourselves fitting into the world. The medieval imagination experienced the self as "porous," embedded in creation, in need of divine protection, and vulnerable to the social, spiritual, and cosmic forces of good and evil. In modernity, we began to picture ourselves as "buffered," making our own decisions in a private, autonomous, mental space from which we gaze out upon a world of objects that can be controlled. These shifts laid significant groundwork for a materialistic view of the world to feel plausible. Even if God was kept in the picture, God's place in the world had shifted. I think we can see traces of these shifts under way in *The London Vocabulary*.

Again, we can ask what kind of world is implied by the choice and sequencing of topics. What comes first and last? (Things and grammar.) What is given more space (objects of various kinds) or less space (ethics, faith, vulnerability)? What is thought worth emphasizing and what is left out? As we move from things to creatures, men, stuff, society, and grammar, what kind of world is evoked?

Imagine yourself a student using this text. It does not look weird to you; the others all have one like it. As far as you know, this is what language textbooks have looked like since the beginning of the world. It is a successful textbook, and it works as far as learning some Latin is concerned. But what else do you learn? What assumptions do you imbibe about what it means to be a good student, to be a good person, to succeed at school? Who are the winners and the losers? For what kind of life do you imagine yourself preparing, and why?

Back in Our Day

Finally, once more leaping recklessly over a lot of intervening history, we turn to *Kontakte*, a present-day language textbook.[8] Recall its opening chapters, "Who I Am and What I Do" and "Possessions and Pleasures."[9] From there, we go on to "Talents, Plans, Obligations," and our memories of vacations and birthdays.[10] We spend two chapters talking about money, work, and accommodation. Food now goes together with eating out, buying groceries, recipes, and shopping for clothes in a chapter titled "Eating and Shopping."[11] There are two chapters on traveling, with a strong emphasis on vacation travel. A chapter on childhood includes stories about childhood experiences and fairy tales. A range of mild ailments and accidents is covered, along with practice at buying remedies at pharmacies and a section on haircuts. The last chapter is titled "Modern Society" and includes treatment of multicultural society, a section on "beloved money," and discussion of art and literature.[12]

Compared to our earlier texts, the natural world has all but disappeared, with scarcely any talk or representation of creatures other than humans. Calamity, death, ethics, virtues, and religion are not noticeable topics.[13] No one dies except in a retelling of *Snow White*. Adjectives describing people tend to refer to appearance rather than character: fat, thin, beautiful, pretty, tall, short, etc. Love is primarily romantic.[14] The images are now stock photos or brief cartoon narratives in which German characters eat, drink, shop, travel, and socialize but do not seem to believe, pray, or suffer.[15] Racial diversity remains fairly minimal.

Once more we can ask: What comes first and last? (Me and modern society.) What is given more space (personal preferences and experiences and consumer behaviors) or less space (other creatures, ethics, faith, vulnerability)? What is thought worth emphasizing and what is left out? As we move from self to experiences, travel, eating, shopping, childhood, illness, and society, what kind of world is evoked?

If you are in this class, this text does not look weird to you. You assume it is just how language textbooks are and always have been. It helps you learn words and grammar. What else do you learn? What assumptions do you imbibe about what it means to be a good student, to be a good person, to succeed at school? Who are the winners and the losers? For what kind of life do you imagine yourself preparing, and why?

Framing Narratives

I have skipped across centuries, briefly summarized complex texts, and focused on some details more than others. I am not offering a detailed history here. I am simply pointing out that while each of these courses teaches words and grammar, none of them is a view from nowhere. Each is a story-shaped journey on which students are invited to embark. The choices and sequences that make up a course progression are invitations to share beliefs and assumptions about the shape of our life in the world. These invitations come to us not through direct preaching but through the implicit curriculum. They are carried in details such as:

- what comes first (orienting us) and last (creating a satisfying whole);
- the sequencing and trajectory of the topics (where are we headed?);
- which topics receive more space and time (what matters most?);
- how topics are named, focusing us on, say, hospitality or on eating and shopping (what is the context?); and
- what is quietly left unmentioned (what can we safely ignore?).

The worldview of each text is carried not just by whether it mentions God but also by how it depicts food, or bodies, or work. It is carried by what is selected from life outside the classroom and whether suffering, mercy, or justice is worth mentioning. Each text likely looks normal to those who share its time, place, and assumptions; some awareness of history can help us see that the way we do things might not be inevitable, however normal it feels. If we ask how our own courses connect to faith only by considering whether we can insert prayer, a Bible reference, or a religious topic, we miss this larger fabric. If we fail to give thought to how the overall story is crafted, we may find ourselves telling someone else's story under the illusion that we are just telling it like it is.

Exercises

- If we removed all direct references to God, religion, and church from all three of the textbooks described here, would they then be equivalent to one another in terms of their relationship to Christian faith? What might we still be able to say about how well each fits with a Christian story about the world?
- Consider a course or sequence that you teach and make a list of the following: What comes first and last? What does the sequence of topics suggest about where we are headed? What receives most time and least time? How do you name topics? What is absent that could have been connected to the course topic? Then consider what your findings suggest in terms of the story offered to students about how this piece of learning fits into the world and how the world fits together.

SHOWING AND HIDING

I was recently in a church service that was themed around care for creation. We began with a striking video montage, and the sermon was accompanied by photographs. The images were calculated to evoke a sense of beauty and wonder, and followed somewhat predictable lines: nebulae, crashing waves, sunsets, forest streams, waterfalls, flowers. At the end of the service, the pastor blessed the congregation and closed with the words: "and now we can go back out into God's creation and enjoy its beauty."

I did not ask, but I strongly suspect the pastor was well aware that we were already in God's creation during the service. Where else would we be? Since we had never left creation, we could hardly go back into it. I wondered how far the images had steered his words. We saw stars and mountains and rivers, but no molecules, or spiders, or buildings, or poems. The images implied that "creation" meant "nature," especially those parts of nature that seem aesthetically pleasing or inspiring. The closing words suggested that once we went outside and saw the blue sky and the flowers, we would be back in creation. I expect the pastor knew that "creation" in Christian theology does not mean "nature," but rather everything that is not God.[1] But the visuals had carried us down a different narrative path in which creation was a container for us outside our meeting, rather than we, our meeting, and everything involved in it being fully part of creation. I wondered to what degree our pictures were influencing our theology.

Most classrooms and learning materials include images of some kind. We can think of these as illustrations, visual aids, accommodation of learner differences, motivators, or aesthetic enhancements, and they can play all of these roles. They are also narrative devices. Like words and sequences, our images act as framing devices, giving learners clues about how they should imagine the topic and the wider world. If we show pictures only of male, Caucasian, or Western scientists, we suggest who should imagine becoming a scientist. If we show pictures in which the people of another country are always rural and poor, we imply something about how that people group is positioned in the world. If we consistently show pictures of waterfalls and flowers while talking about creation, we imply a way of thinking about that doctrine.

Since we already have some context, I propose to return one last time to the *Orbis Pictus* and *The London Vocabulary*, but this time focusing on the pictures. We have taken a peek into the story structure implicit in each text. What do the pictures add to the implicit curriculum?

Birds

The *Orbis Pictus* includes six chapters on birds and groups them according to their habitats, including the chapter shown here on aquatic birds.[2] The text tells us their names and also describes a few of their behaviors, the beauty of their song, or how they find food. Comenius believed that education should represent creatures as invitations to love and responsible care.[3] Part of wisdom is learning to delight in creation. Another part is learning how to handle our power over other creatures in light of every creature's desire to flourish, for "all creatures should have cause to praise God with us (Psalm 148)."[4] If we want to learn to live well with other creatures, we need to see them living in the contexts in which they thrive.

The London Vocabulary has a single chapter on birds.[5] The habitats have disappeared, as has the description of birds' behaviors. Various birds appear in parallel rows against a blank background, accompanied by the image of a person who traps them for a living.[6] There are no clues regarding what the birds need to live. Beneath the image is simply a list of bird species. James Greenwood explains in the preface that he has reduced the "vast heap of words" in earlier books to a list of those needed for navigating good classical authors.[7] We need a list of Latin bird words because birds were mentioned by the Romans, and reading the Romans makes us well educated. Questions about how birds fit into our world or whether we have responsibilities toward them have faded. The beaks and feathers remain, but the story has changed, and that is echoed in the picture.

(ABOVE) ORBIS PICTUS: BIRDS

(BELOW) THE LONDON VOCABULARY: BIRDS

Food

The *Orbis Pictus* has many chapters on food, ranging from agriculture through food preparation to a culminating chapter on a shared meal, depicted in the picture below.[8] Notice the guest being welcomed at the door in the background on the right, and the water provided at the far right for the guest to wash their hands before joining others at the communal table. In the foreground on the right the host pours water into a bowl for the guest and provides a towel. All of these details are described in the text, which concludes with the host drinking a toast to their guests. The meal is framed by a focus on hospitality.

In *The London Vocabulary* (see the picture on p. 96), those who grow and prepare food are gone, and there is one chapter listing foods.[9] A party of conspicuously well-dressed people converse at the table while a servant, with whom no one is making eye contact, pours drinks. We need to learn to name the foods listed below the picture, but we are not invited to reflect on where they came from or on how to be hospitable. Food apparently comes into existence at the end of the servant's arm. The table, dishes, and waiter remain, but the image tells a different story.

ORBIS PICTUS: THE SHARED MEAL

THE LONDON VOCABULARY: MEATS AND DRINKS

Ships

The *Orbis Pictus* depicts ships several times, including in a late chapter on naval warfare (see the first picture on p. 97). To the right of the image, ships exchange cannon fire. To the left, in the background, a ship's powder magazine has exploded, and fragments of ship and crew fly mingled through the billowing smoke. In the front left corner, a ship is sinking. Two sailors on deck, most likely at that time in history unable to swim, raise their arms to heaven in supplication. Just to the right of the foundering ship, an individual already drowning in the ocean does the same. "A sea fight is terrible," the text warns, before tersely and vividly describing the terrors involved.[10]

In the equivalent chapter in *The London Vocabulary* (see the second picture on p. 97), the ship floats serenely on the waves.[11] We memorize words for the parts of the ship and move on. Ships are technical creations, surely not implicated in our hostilities, cruelties, and calamities. The image underscores a tendency in *The London Vocabulary* to edit out anything associated with sin, suffering, or death. The reader/viewer is positioned as a dispassionate observer of a well-ordered world.

(ABOVE) ORBIS PICTUS: A SEA BATTLE

(BELOW) THE LONDON VOCABULARY: OF SEA OR NAVAL AFFAIRS

Pictures and Perspectives

Each pair of pictures shares a similar explicit curriculum. They announce that we are about to learn words associated with birds, food, and ships, and they provide those words. This layer of meaning, the information to be covered, is the one we tend to most immediately have in mind when we plan what to teach.

Each pair of pictures also reflects an implicit curriculum, and here they diverge. Each reflects assumptions about how the world works, what matters, what learners should notice, and how they should grow. Those assumptions leak through in the way the material is visualized. Though the differences might seem small, the second picture of each pair nudges us away from seeing the world as morally shaped, narratively ordered, and oriented toward love and accountability. We are nudged toward seeing the world as a collection of objects under the gaze of a privileged observer. The narrative inclusions, absences, and sequences discussed in the last chapter already suggest this, but the worldview is not just in the words. The message is reinforced by the pictures.

Both texts are of course quite old and distant from our own classrooms. Yet as I study them and then turn back to current language textbooks on my own shelf, I do so with fresh eyes. I notice that today birds (and nonhuman creatures in general) have disappeared almost completely. The word "bird" appears in the glossary, but we learn the names of no specific kinds of birds. The only bird images I can find in one book are cartoon pictures of chickens dressed as tourists. The absence seems both haunting and telling when we reflect that long-term surveys in North America show "a net loss in total abundance of 2.9 billion birds across almost all biomes, a reduction of 29% since 1970."[12] Food is pictured in restaurants and supermarkets, means of travel are depicted in connection with vacations, and the only dangers to life and limb are those that can be resolved at the pharmacy. Present in abundance are cartoon images of humans engaging in leisure activities and various forms of consumption. In my classroom too, the worldview is not just in the words.

There is no way to include everything in a course, so we have to make choices. Every picture, even a photograph, is created from a vantage point that shows some things and hides others. When the presences and absences start to add up into a pattern across the various images in our courses, they become a story offered to our students. If the main point is to learn food vocabulary, or words for parts of ships, then skipping over the existence of farm laborers or warfare may just be temporary expediency. Yet it may also become an act of framing that adds up over time. There is no simple formula for getting our choice of images right. But we can meaningfully ask whether the way we depict the world nests plausibly inside the larger story of a God of mercy reconciling a fractured world and calling us to a wholeness grounded in love.

In FRAMING, we have considered framing words, sequences, and images. The pictures, sequences, and words work together. The way discourses are connected or separated (is computer programming connected to hospitality?), the way learning is named (do we learn to speak or hear a language?), the way material is ordered (do we start with wisdom or things? Do we end with the day of judgment or beloved money?), the pictures we use (birds in habitats or pinned in rows), and the absences where things have been omitted (welcomes, workers, suffering)—all of these conspire together to project a story about how things are. We can think about these one by one, and it can be helpful to do so. Our students experience the whole.

Exercises

- None of the pictures discussed in this chapter include crosses, churches, or Bibles. So what bearing do Christian concerns have on each of them? How might your theology of creation, of hospitality, or of suffering affect how you view each picture?
- How do you habitually think about the images that appear in your classroom (on a screen, in a textbook, on worksheets, on wall displays)? Is choosing them a thoughtful part of your preparation? Do you think of this as part of integrating faith and learning? Why/why not?
- Choose a sequence you teach and collect all the images that students will see while you are teaching it. Make notes on what they show (what is included in the representation?), what they hide (what is not shown that could be relevant to your learning goals?), and what story they might be telling (what do they imply matters most?).

ASSIGNING

LOOKING FOR ANSWERS

All teachers assign tasks. We tell students orally or in writing what to read, what to write, what to find out, what to get done by next week. Those communications likely represent a relatively small portion of our time, but they have a large impact on how students use their time. Telling students what to do next is an everyday activity, routine and mundane. What could it have to do with being Christian?

One of the gifts of research projects that involve focus groups with students is the chance to listen closely to how they describe their learning processes. Part of one conversation with students has stayed with me for some time and challenged my classroom practices. As we talked about their experiences of learning with digital technologies in school, two students reflected aloud about what happens when their teachers assign reading tasks:

> [Student 1]: we'll ask [our teachers], "can we skim it and just look for the answers?" And they're, like, "No, I actually want you to read it." . . . One of my teachers did that and I diligently read it and took notes . . . because I just do that. And I know a lot of people did because he emphasized that it's important to read it, whereas most teachers I get, I kind of skim it and look for the answers.
>
> [Student 2]: they just say, "Here's your reading assignment, fill out the worksheet," and it is easy to just do Apple F [i.e., to use the computer search function] and find where the answers are to each of the questions.[1]

What first intrigued me was the sense of internal tension in these comments. The students offer two contrasting narratives about their experience, narratives that sit quite uneasily alongside each other.

First, we hear a gratifying story of consistently attentive, ethically attuned teachers and habitually virtuous students. In this story, teachers in general ("they") are in the habit of emphasizing that they "actually want you to read it." Careful reading and reflection matter to them. They make time as a matter of course to engage students in thinking about how they will read, not just what they will read. The students in turn read the text carefully and take notes, simply because that's the kind of engaged, diligent learners they are: "I just do that." Great teachers, great students, great learning. What could go wrong?

The second story is woven through the gaps in the first, and in this version the skies are darker, the road less straight. Here it was just "one of my teachers" who offered specific guidance about how to read, not all of them. It turns out that when "most teachers I get" assign tasks, they just say "here's your reading assignment." The task is framed less as a targeted opportunity for growth and more as an obligation to get something done. In this scenario, with the messaging focused on task completion, we suddenly find that the supposedly diligent student does not read so carefully after all. In most instances, "I kind of skim it and look for the answers."

Conflicted Stories

There are likely several things going on in the tension between these two stories about learning. I suspect that most of us like to entertain stories about ourselves that make us seem more virtuous than the balance of our actual daily choices might warrant. We want to think that we are good people, and so we tell ourselves that we generally are, overgeneralizing our best moments (unless we are in that self-accusing frame of mind that overgeneralizes all of our worst moments). We also internalize the expectations of others who matter to us, and it becomes tempting to tell our story in ways that we think might meet those expectations. And we often look for the shortest path to satisfying the many demands on us amid busy lives and competing desires. It seems likely that these students, who admit to frequently skimming for answers instead of reading, are finding that their strategy is successful at meeting what their teachers seem to want and getting them through their day without feeling too lost. If that weren't the case, we might hear more about struggle and failure rather than a story about how easy it is to get things done.

Such interior negotiations take place in a context. In this case, digital devices and the persistent tug of their most easily adopted patterns of usage are in play. The students note that digital technology (the search function on their Apple devices) amplifies the temptation to default to skim reading because it makes that mode of engagement easy. Just as the existence of a convenient and simple copy-paste function increases the ease of plagiarism,[2] easily accessible search functions make it easier to just search for the sentences that contain the answers. If the assignment implies that what is needed is really just answers to assigned questions, searching saves all the trouble of reading and understanding the text. As long as the answers turn out to be mostly correct, it is likely to be a winning strategy, at least in the short term. Who among us does not take shortcuts that get us results?

If what is desired also includes growing skill at understanding extended arguments, an awareness of context, or a grasp of how pieces of information meaningfully fit together, it becomes less clear that this particular shortcut helps us. The barriers to achieving something that looks like a kind of success without full engagement or deep learning have been lowered by digital tools. Less disciplined forms of reading become the path of least resistance, and defaulting to skimming and scanning strategies becomes more likely. It then requires an explicit intervention by the teacher ("because he emphasized") for students to consider deeper engagement. Just saying "here's your reading assignment" may be an even less effective gambit than it used to be. If these students are offering competing accounts of their learning experience, how much of this might be rooted in living up to mixed messages from their teachers about the point of doing the assignment?

We can continue to expand the context. The school where this conversation took place was in the United States. Teachers and students in this part of the world (and in many other locations shaped by modernity) are living in a task-oriented culture that offers more pressure toward getting as many things as possible done than toward deep reflection. Research suggests the presence in our makeup (at least in this cultural context) of a "completion bias."[3] We have learned to derive satisfaction from completing and checking off tasks, to the degree that simply checking off a few quick and easy tasks at the start of each day can increase our overall motivation and sense of satisfaction. This bias can lead us to prefer easier tasks that lead to a quick sense of completion and to avoid, procrastinate on, or devote fewer mental resources to more challenging and complex tasks. The practices of schooling feed into this when we assign and assess tasks in ways that foreground completion as an end in itself rather than the learning that the tasks are meant to foster.[4] When we communicate tasks with a primary focus on quantity and deadline ("read to page 37," "answer 8 questions," "write 200 words," "get it read by Tuesday," "here's your reading assignment, fill out the worksheet") and do not balance this with an explicit focus on what kind of learning is intended, we invite students to focus more on productivity than growth.

This is, of course, not a zero-sum game. Sometimes a focus on getting things done might be a legitimate emphasis and a necessary skill to develop. Sometimes we do need students to get to page 37. Yet if learners come to sense a pattern of emphasis in their teachers' demands that portrays compliance and productivity as the key markers of success, it should not be surprising that shortcuts to producing answers without much reflection become even more tempting. The quantity of work assigned can be a factor here too. One of my students with a heavy humanities course load reflected in a journal entry that "having almost 200–300 pages of reading each night makes it quite literally impossible for me to read in a leisurely way," leading to a loss of the satisfaction she normally found in reading.[5] Here again we can sense that this may not just be about students failing to be virtuous. Teachers are implicated.

What interests me most in all of this is the meaning that students are finding in what, from the teacher's point of view, are probably unexamined moments. I suspect, if my own experience is any guide, that our choices about how to verbally frame learning tasks are often taken without much conscious reflection, especially when we are assigning homework. I suspect that "here's your reading assignment" is more often a last-minute verbal reflex than a carefully considered intervention. It is most often articulated in the last hundred seconds of the class period, when the time allotted for in-class activity has overrun a little, students are beginning to pack away their things, and the instructor is in a slight rush to make sure that the homework gets mentioned so that the juggernaut of the semester can lumber on. I suspect that when we take time to think about faith and learning, student formation, and Christian values and commitments, the moments when we assign homework tasks are not at the top of our list of things to consider. Announcing the assignment is rarely our most reflective moment. Yet it is one of the moments in which we signal what we believe to be important.

This returns us to the need to become explicit about the hopes that frame our semesters. If we have hopes for how students will grow intellectually, socially, ethically, and spiritually, articulating these in a syllabus or opening statement is just the beginning. Think back to the hopes expressed in the syllabi I discussed earlier (p. 30). I offered examples of how I signaled my desire for a kind of reading that sought to grow in charity, humility, patience, and care with the words of others. I was interested in how reading intersects with loving our neighbor, valuing truth, and growing in virtue. If humility, patience, or care is genuinely part of the learning that I am seeking to foster, how well will my learning goals be served by reinforcing a habit of using shortcuts to skim-read for answers to win points? If my reading assignments can be satisfied with a quick list of answers, and if I give those assignments in a way that suggests that what I most care about is the word count covered by Thursday, then it is quite likely that my practices are directly undermining my hopes.

If we care about how students are being formed, and not just about how much they are getting done, we need to attend carefully to the tasks we design and to the messages we send when we assign them. If the task is reading, we will want to regularly talk with students about how they are reading, and not just what they are reading. We will take time to explicitly relate smaller tasks to the bigger story we want to tell students about why we are learning. At least some of the time, that will help students invest differently when they work on the task. Students have their own vices, but they also take cues from us about what they should be trying to become. Assigning homework involves taming our tongue.

Exercises

- Why should Christian educators care if students habitually use shortcuts to productivity? Are there Christian reasons to be concerned about how students read? Do those reasons evaporate if it turns out that those who are not Christian can share similar concerns about reading? Discuss these questions with a colleague.

- Think back over recent classes you have taught in which you assigned tasks at the end of the class session. Write down examples of what you said. Reflect on what was emphasized and what was not said. What might students be inferring about your priorities?
- Write down examples of faith-grounded hopes that you have for your students' learning. Write out examples of weaving these into the way you describe and justify tasks to students. Practice saying them aloud to increase the chance that they will be available to you when you are flustered.

HERE'S YOUR ASSIGNMENT

There are many assignments other than reading, but let's stay with reading for a little longer. The last chapter focused on unintended messages sent when we announce reading assignments. How might we craft more intentional messages?

When I started asking myself not just what but how I wanted students to read, I embarked on a journey through Christian writing about reading. I found one recent elaboration of that long-running conversation particularly suggestive.[1] Paul Griffiths contrasts religious reading (what religious people do when they read sacred texts well) and consumer reading (what we do with the news, the cheap novel, or the restaurant menu). You may want to pause for a moment before reading on, and think for yourself about the distinction. What are the differences in how we go about reading and what the reading does to us?

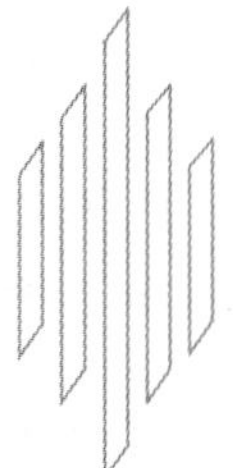

In religious reading, Griffiths says, we read repeatedly and sustain our engagement over time, returning to the same texts for additional layers of meaning. We discipline ourselves to read attentively, and to read all of the text, even the dry parts. We give weight to every detail and check our interpretations repeatedly against the text. We read in community, both in study groups and in conversation with past readers; it still matters what Augustine or Hildegard said about the text. We come with a basic reverence, an expectation that even when we do not immediately understand, the text has truth that we lack. We hope for personal change through our encounter with the text.

In consumer reading, we typically read once, we read swiftly, and as soon as we are done, the text is disposable. Once the information or entertainment has been extracted, we donate the novel, recycle the magazine, return the menu. The text was instrumental to what we wanted to get out of it, not something with its own enduring value. We read individually, looking for what is relevant to our own interests; if we want to go straight to the comics and others want the sports pages, that's fine. Imposing our own idiosyncratic interpretations or skipping sections we don't need are not moral failings here. We remain in charge of the process, with little expectation of our souls being laid bare and little invested in the authority of the text.

Of course, these are ideal types. Texts have various degrees of weightiness, and our actual acts of reading fall somewhere along a continuum. How do we read C. S. Lewis, or Shakespeare, or our favorite culinary guru? Do we ever read the Bible as if it were a recipe book, a fortune cookie, or an encyclopedia? Note also that the lesson is not that religious reading is good and consumer reading bad. Forming study groups to engage in meditative memorization of restaurant menus would not be a sensible response. Rapidly scanning for information and extracting quick answers is an important life skill, appropriate in its place, and should be part of our learning.

The point, then, is not to squeeze all reading into two narrow boxes or to discard one end of the continuum. A better question is whether we are better at one kind of reading than the other, and why.[2] In a culture focused on rapid consumption of digital media largely funded and framed by advertising, our consumer reading abilities develop quickly. Are we also growing in our capacity for deep, sustained, repeated, careful engagement? If not, what are the consequences for our formation, for our faith, for the church?

With that brief sketch of some of Griffiths's concerns in mind, let's return to teaching. If an imbalance toward consumer reading is a problem, are the reading assignments given in school helping or hindering?[3] If I start out, as in the sample syllabus I provided earlier (p. 30), telling students that I would like us to focus on learning to read with humility, patience, charity, and justice, I signal that it will matter not only that we get the texts read but also what kinds of readers we are becoming. If this is to be more than a brave opening flourish, I then need to attend to how I design and communicate tasks. I will need, for instance, to avoid overreliance on tasks and assessments that might steer us toward skim reading, summaries, and quick searches for answers. I will need to find ways not just of getting my students to read, but of getting them to think about what is happening while they are reading. If my assignments are not plausible steps in the direction of the hopes that I have articulated, those hopes become mostly hot air.

Framing Tasks

There are many ways to frame reading assignments, and we can only explore a few examples here. Mark Schwehn, for instance, describes how one of his students combined insightful commentary on *King Lear* with reexamination of a fractured relationship in her own life. The connections made by the student led him to reconsider his assignments. As he describes the process:

> I had always asked questions like, "How does Norman Maclean order the complicated story of Young Men and Fire so as to provide consolation for himself and his readers?" Or, "Why is it so important to Maclean that he be able actually to find a story in Mann Gulch instead of simply inventing one or imposing one upon the materials he has discovered?" But I now added discussion or examination questions like the following: "How do Maclean's intricate and extended imaginative efforts to come to terms with a 'natural catastrophe' strengthen your resourcefulness in coming to terms with natural catastrophes in your own life, including disease and death?"[4]

He explains that he was not just trying to make texts "relevant." He wanted to "enlarge and strengthen the students' imaginations so that they could in turn be more imaginative in their efforts to remedy wrongs, mend broken relationships, or otherwise advance human flourishing."[5] The changes he made were quite small, but "small course alterations (pun intended) at the beginning can yield very different destinations at the conclusion of a journey."[6]

In my own courses, I have similarly experimented with shifting the implied focus of reflection. "Analyze how Heinrich Böll uses Christian imagery to critique Nazi ideology" produces different writing from "Write a letter to a thoughtful Christian friend explaining how reading Böll's story carefully could constructively inform their life." Some of the information students need to cite might be the same, but the task has a different purpose and a wider relational context. None of this implies that we should not spend time focusing on the text for its own sake. It is more a matter of considering what kinds of engagement with a text might be implied by our hopes for student formation.

Another relevant factor is where and when the task might be completed. In a literature course, I have asked students to take a short text and try reading it lying on their bed, then in an armchair, then sitting upright at a table, and reflect on whether anything changed in their ability to focus and read carefully. We discussed their findings in class with explicit reference to how we might foster the ability to read charitably, patiently, and justly.

Reading also has a relational context. Many assignments assume that reading outside class will be done alone and in silence, but reading can and should also be practiced aloud and with others. A reading could be summarized or key sentences read aloud to a friend.[7] Interesting passages or challenging ideas could be discussed with a family member. Having intermediate language students read fables in German and then write their own versions to be used in literacy work in a middle school classroom in Switzerland not only turned my students' language work into an act of service but generated engaging letters back to my undergraduate students from the Swiss children. ("Your story started out well but then became boring," wrote one. "But don't worry, my writing does not always go well either.") We still practiced grammar, but now other goods were in play.

In one course I drew from Mark Pike's research on secondary school students reading poetry.[8] He found some students consistently looking for a poem to give them a feeling, while others wanted a puzzle to solve, a big idea to contemplate, or just a task to get done. I asked my students to reflect on which of Pike's reader types most resembled their own approach to the poems we were reading. The point, however, was not to focus on their own preferences. I asked them to think about how their own inclinations and limitations related to reading in community. Which poems seem a good fit for me, and how might I therefore need the help of other readers for those poems I find harder to access? Perhaps the humility to realize that an apparently unrewarding text is speaking to someone else could draw us into listening more closely to one another's interpretations.

This kind of consideration is not only relevant to the literature classroom. An assigned science reading could be accompanied by a neighborhood walk with a relative looking for examples of what the reading is scientifically describing.[9] A reading about politics might be accompanied by a conversation with a local community leader about the same themes.[10] In a class on *Life Together*, Dietrich Bonhoeffer's theological account of Christian community as intentional fellowship even with those who do not gratify us, I asked students to choose a person who irritated them and express thankfulness for their life once a day for a week. The assignment led both to thoughtful reflection on their own reactions to others and to a deeper appreciation for what Bonhoeffer was getting at in his text.[11]

Hopes and Tasks

We could go on listing possible permutations of reading assignments, but the point here is not just variety or finding new paths to student engagement. The point is designing assignments that match our hopes. In place of the invitation to cover the ground implied by "here's your reading assignment," a carefully articulated task becomes a chance to remind ourselves who we are trying to become as we read. We could devote the same kind of reflection to tasks focused on other skills, such as writing, research, or artistic creation. How might we learn to write charitably and justly about others? How is humility implicated in the wording of a research report? What is the role of patience or courage in the process of artistic creation? With any assignment, it matters whether the task genuinely contributes to mastering basic course skills and ideas. We do want to cover the ground. Yet it also matters how the assignment invites us to engage.

As a response to reading this chapter, I suggest a kind of spiritual discipline for a current or future semester. Here's your assignment:

Once a week, when you announce an assignment to students, take the time to say a little about:

- how you want them to engage in the assignment,
- how you think that engagement will help them to grow, and
- why you think that.

Connect the assignment to the deeper hopes you have for your class. Share your own learning experiences and articulate your hopes for students. Communicate a vision that involves more than productivity. Name what is supposed to change for the better because we completed this assignment. Give students a vision to frame the task.

I am making no assumption here that if we just get the words right, all students will respond virtuously or that the challenges of learning will be vanquished. I am not offering one more strategy for increasing productivity and control. This is not a tip for getting more students to do the reading.

Then why do it? First, because students need a vision to sustain their labor and are influenced by what teachers tell them about their learning. Avoiding busywork, articulating hope, and naming how we think students can grow are acts of care, the kind of care that goes to the heart of what teachers are there for.[12] Care taken with task articulation is love of neighbor. Second, because the mere attempt forces us into explicit reflection on our own practices and pushes us toward integrity and consistency. It might help nudge us further into the mundane habit of letting faith and learning indwell the same trains of thought. These twin impulses of care and integrity are, I think, enough to make it worth devoting some uncomfortable attention to how we assign things.

Exercises

- Return to the first exercise from the last chapter, which asked: Are there Christian reasons to be concerned about how students read? Have the examples in this chapter provided any ways of extending your answer?

- Look back at the weekly assignment described in the last part of this chapter. Choose one assignment per week for each of the next several weeks and write out a short account of how you hope students will approach it, how you hope they will grow, and why. Reflect on how this assignment relates to your broader hopes for student formation, your beliefs about how to live well, and the mission of your school. Then introduce the assignment to students in a manner based on your plan. Don't make it a theatrical occasion, just announce the assignment with forethought.
- Invite a few students for a shared lunch. Consider whether students not currently in your class might feel freer to share ideas with you. Ask them to talk about how they approach their homework assignments, what they sense their teachers are looking for, and whether any assignments have nudged them to engage in a more focused or transformative way. See what you can learn, bearing in mind that you may have to repeat the exercise a few times with different students before you can begin to sense general trends.

TEACHERS AND BURDENS

When designed well, assignments create opportunities for learning. They also create burdens. I am writing this paragraph between end-of-semester meetings with individual students who are describing the stresses of projects from multiple classes all due in the same week. Yesterday I was communicating with a student who had fallen behind about a plan to catch up. I just read a student's journal in which she reflects on how the volume of work from her current combination of classes is eroding her capacity to take joy in learning. The work of teachers creates burdens for students, sometimes heavy ones.

The burdens themselves are not necessarily a problem. Students should work hard at learning, provided the work is genuinely learning. In a healthy institution, they should be able to do so with various kinds of support and encouragement. Yet the extent of my impact on students' lives outside the classroom leads me to wonder how the assignments I design affect students' ability to thrive.

In the last chapter I summarized Paul Griffiths's distinction between reading that seeks efficient access to information and gratification and reading that opens us to transformation. Thinking about this some years ago while redesigning a literature course led me to focus on the question of burdens.[1]

It seemed to me that for most of the texts we were reading, a quick read before class to avoid being caught unprepared was not the right mode of engagement. I worried that my assignments sometimes encouraged shortcuts. I wanted to foster more sustained engagement and a conscious focus on reading charitably. An obvious next step was to reason that it is hard to read charitably if you read everything only once. I chose three short stories and made space in the course to assign each one twice, giving us an opportunity to dig deeper than our first reading would allow.

The problem now was that I was asking for more. I was already asking my students to read difficult texts in a language not their own, to be willing to risk speaking about them in that language, to write reflections, and to keep up with a brisk course schedule alongside the demands of their other professors, the job funding their studies, the place on the swim team, the volunteering at church, and the need to have a social life. Now I also wanted them to reflect more deeply on their reading process and to read the same text carefully more than once. I wanted them to think of reading as an arena for virtue and vice, for the exercise of charity and justice, for working out our faith. I could sense the jaws of a trap. Was this just a desire for my students to be more righteous than I ever was as a student? Might an itch to point a finger at some bracing virtues and to stir my students to their ardent pursuit risk simply ratcheting up the pressure?

Jesus spoke directly about teachers and burdens. He spoke of those who embrace the role of teaching others how to live and yet do so from a safe distance. "They tie up heavy burdens, hard to bear, and lay them on the shoulders of others; but they themselves are unwilling to lift a finger to move them" (Matt. 23:4 NRSV). The image evokes a willingness to watch others struggle to meet standards of righteousness that we can't be bothered to meet ourselves. These teachers had "multiplied the ways in which we can offend God but not helped others to please God," resulting in a process of "imposing regulations without giving relief."[2] Jesus invites us to think about the demands we make of others in the context of solidarity and the flourishing of our neighbor. He spoke elsewhere of a yoke and a burden still present, yet offered in gentleness and humility (Matt. 11:28–30).

I didn't want to simply multiply demands. When I asked students to read the first story for the second time, we had already begun to talk about reading with justice, charity, and humility. I was now asking them to test their capacity for such reading by engaging in a second careful reading of a text they had already read and discussed at length in class. My students typically report that they have rarely, if ever, been asked to do such a thing; texts in school get assigned once. I knew that there would be a temptation to fall back on memory and skip or speed up the second reading.

One of my strategies for addressing that temptation was shameless pleading. You already know, I reminded them, that one of our goals this semester is to figure out what it might look like to read with charity, with patience, with justice and humility, to read in a way framed by the call to love. We will not get far if we only engage in fly-by reading. If our time is to be invested well, if we are going to have a chance of doing what we say we are doing, I need you to find a quiet place and read this story again. I know that you are going to be tempted to skip a task that does not feel like getting more done. But if we don't do this, the whole project leaves the rails. Will you commit to this, at least this once? Please?

My students are thoughtful and gracious people, and most would have responded to the request alone. But I feared that exhortation unsupported by structure could lead mostly to increased guilt. I had increased the stakes without adding support. The pressures on my students' time would not evaporate in the face of the sincerity of my appeals. When those pressures won out, "I didn't get to the homework" would now have escalated to "I am a bad person."

I added a second strategy. I looked for a task that involved spotting and reporting on fresh details. Find all the places where the author uses a color adjective, and come to class with some thoughts about the patterns and what they might be communicating. The point was to provide a meaningful task that was impossible to complete from memory. I also assigned a journaling task in which students reflected on what went well or poorly in their reading process. I hoped that the combination of a focused task, the expectation of sharing the results with others, and reporting on the process significantly increased the likelihood that the second reading would in fact happen. The journal task also meant that even if it did not go well, that would still give students something to contribute.

The combination mattered. Exhortation without structure feels uncomfortably close to Jesus's description of burdens imposed without help. Giving a detail-finding task to force rereading without articulating the larger purpose easily lapses into extra busywork and behavioral conformity. If we could structure our work so that it might get done and at the same time have a clear shared story about the larger goals in play, perhaps the language of virtue could invite growth and not merely impose added burdens.

When we came together to discuss our rereading, I clustered the chairs in the middle of the room and sat among the students as a way of gathering around the text. We discussed their findings. Then I described how I had read the story multiple times, surveyed much of the secondary literature, and taught the text several times. Then one day, a year or two earlier, as I was reading it again in preparation for class, I suddenly noticed a pattern in the imagery that I had never seen before, one that had significant consequences for what we think the story is about. With all the expertise I had gleaned up to that point, and despite the several times I had read the text, I had completely missed it. My students had not spotted it either. We turned back to the text to see if I might be right.

My intent was to position myself alongside my students as one also learning to read well. I too am learning to have enough patience for truth to emerge and enough charity and humility to let the text have meanings that I have not yet mastered. I wanted it to be visible that I was not preaching patient reading while teaching from last year's notes. I wanted to avoid preaching humility while modeling confident mastery. On the terms of Jesus's image, I was trying to lift a finger.

I tried to sustain this pattern across the semester, combining explicit vision with concrete strategies for living into it together. I doubt that I always succeeded. I did take courage from the degree to which students' journals suggested that they found the struggle constructive, fruitful, even transformative.

Burdens and Barriers

Another reason to think carefully about student burdens became vivid for me some years ago when I was helping a refugee family from Burundi to learn English. One day their teenage daughter asked for help with her math homework. She had been struggling to achieve good scores on the problems assigned for homework and needed help with the latest set. I could sympathize; math was never a school subject in which I felt particularly at home. Yet as we talked through the word problems on the worksheet, it became clear the difficulty did not lie where I thought it did. As we tackled problems based on scenarios such as Joe working out at the gym, it became apparent that she was actually very, very good at mental arithmetic, but that her cultural experience did not include things like gym memberships. She was trying to understand math problems framed in her third language and built around unfamiliar concepts and behaviors. The difficult shaded into the ridiculous when we reached a problem based on how many gifts the Grinch stole from each house in Whoville. Her scores on such tasks were less a reflection of her success at math than of her struggle to decode unfamiliar cultural narratives.

Here again, the surprise is not that learning creates burdens, or that different students struggle to differing degrees. It is that the task as designed creates specific barriers for some students, making it harder for them to make progress. Those barriers can come in various forms. If I assign tasks requiring significant collaboration and do not assign time in class for groups to work on them, I favor those students who can most easily get together outside class. Their ability to do so may be affected by factors such as their place of residence and access to transportation, their job schedules and income needs, the strength of their social connections, or their involvement in sports or volunteer programs, none of which are things I should be assessing when I grade their work. If I create tests that rely heavily on one type of test item, I am likely to favor the students who do best at that kind of item. If I present content at high speed, then those who need a slower pace to be able to process it well, such as those not working in their first language, are likely to suffer disproportionately. If I design activities without attending to the needs of students with differing levels of, say, visual acuity or mobility, I reduce access to learning for some. And so on.[3] There will always be differences among students, including how long it might take them to complete a task, what background they bring, or how difficult they might find it. But we need to be careful to identify what we are really assessing and whose difficulties we are multiplying when we assign a task.

As I have worked at designing a brand-new course this year, my mind has been on burdens and who lifts a finger to move them. As I design assignments, how can I challenge students to grow while providing the support that might nurture that growth, communicating gentleness and humility, and attending to the variety of student needs? How do I reach for deep hopes for students' formation without creating fresh barriers? I don't think the solution is to lower my sights. I want to stretch students, to draw them into ways of engaging that they had not anticipated. But I also want to keep probing for lightness and solidarity in the burdens, for the yoke that at least sometimes feels like grace.

Exercises

- Review the major assignments that you have given to students this semester or this year. Complete the sentences:
    - This assignment is easiest for students who . . .
    - This assignment is hardest for students who . . .
    - This assignment creates hurdles for students who . . .
    - This assignment could support students in their different circumstances by . . .
- The examples in this part of the book have drawn heavily from reading assignments and from courses in which reading is a major part of the work. Choose another type of student task (writing, problem solving, research, etc.) and design an assignment for it that reflects the concerns raised in these chapters. For instance, instead of charitable, patient reading, it could focus on writing in a way that honors others, responding artistically or scientifically to the beauty of the world with gratitude, thinking about how others are represented in images, or something else. Collaborate with a colleague on this or share the result with a colleague for feedback.

PAUSING

SMALL PAUSES

None of us teach without pause or at a consistently even pace. The texture of teaching and learning is peppered with hesitations, silences, reflective moments, things lingered over. Inevitably, teaching means moving through time, but that movement is not just reckoned in minutes. It has eloquent rhythms that become part of the landscape of learning.

Most teachers are aware that the physical landscape plays a role in learning. As I begin writing this chapter, I am sitting in a room on my campus that bears the label "creative agency suite." Cushioned, flexible chairs with wheels are gathered around three small, vaguely oval tables. An L-shaped sofa faces two floor cushions. An enormous digital screen dominates one wall. The center of the room contains an empty space larger than I am used to seeing in classrooms. Someone has worked hard to make the furniture here say, "slow down, you are supposed to be creative here."

Just beyond the glass wall are a coffee kiosk and a tight cluster of high tables with tall, hard-top stools that whisper: "chat, but don't linger." A little farther away, some students sit on bench seats in booths communing with laptops; others chat in armchairs around low coffee tables. Two doors down the corridor, a classroom space is packed to capacity with perfectly straight rows of hard plastic chairs. Each has a small, individual writing surface attached to one side. All face an instructor's desk and a whiteboard. The message of "just listen to the lecture and take notes" seems almost audible.

Physical space encodes messages and affects our behavior. In schools as in restaurants, the furniture, its comfort level and placement, the size of the spaces, and the presence or absence of devices tell us where we are and who we are supposed to be. Picture an expensive restaurant and a sports bar, and the behaviors nurtured in each. Before a word is spoken, we receive messages about what is expected of us, how we can expect those around us to behave, how fast we should move, and what we should treat as important. The physical spaces in which we work and learn are not just a mathematical puzzle of how to fit this many objects into that many square meters. They are an ongoing conversation about who we want to be. Our worldview lives in our furniture, and the chairs are doing a little of the teaching.

It is just as fundamental to our experience of learning that it happens in time.[1] Learning environments speed us up and slow us down, rush us past some things while parking us in front of others. The temporal rhythms in which we work and learn are not just a mathematical puzzle of how to fit this many nuggets of information into that many minutes. They are an ongoing conversation about who we want to be. I wonder how often we think about time as a way of communicating our beliefs and values?[2]

Hope and Response

Let's start very small.

Think of the times during a teaching hour when you are in front of a class, interacting with students, and you pause momentarily.

Now narrow this down specifically to two kinds of pauses. One is the moment that starts when you have just asked a question and ends when the next utterance begins. It is the time from the moment when your last syllable dies in the air to the first sound from a student in response. Early research on this pause dubbed it "wait time 1."[3] The names we give to things can affect how we think about them; here I am going to call this kind of pause the "pause of hope." It is the moment when you hope that students will reward your question with some serious thinking or a helpful answer. If you are met with silence, at a certain point you give up hope of getting an answer and the pause ends as you repeat the question or say something new. The other kind of pause ("wait time 2") begins the moment a student has answered your question or offered a comment, and you are gathering yourself to reply or move on. It is the moment just before you recover your own forward momentum by verbally taking charge again. Let's call it the "pause of response."

These pauses are not just elapsed ticks of the clock. The pause of hope may be accompanied by an expectant expression, a raised eyebrow, a slight forward inclination of the body, a half turn to the board with writing implement raised. I often find myself taking a half step back, unconsciously signaling space for students to take over. These are bodily signals of hope that student engagement will interrupt a potentially awkward silence. A barren wait may undermine my sense of being competent, interesting, or comprehensible. Swift engagement lets me feel as if I am making learning happen, perhaps I am not a fraud after all. If the class hums along, I may hardly notice the gap itself, and so if I do notice it, it may be with the negative connotations of an awkward lag.

Mary Budd Rowe pioneered research on these two pauses in the context of science education.[4] The American science teachers that Rowe studied often hesitated for less than one second during either kind of pause. Training teachers to increase the duration of their wait time improved students' thinking, use of language, and quality of participation. If teachers could be trained to exceed 2.7 seconds, then student responses became three to seven times longer and showed better use of evidence, logic, and speculative thinking. Fewer students failed to respond, disciplinary issues faded, a wider range of students participated, and student confidence and achievement grew. Longer pauses also changed teachers. They became better at interacting with students, asked better questions, and began to expect more of minority students. Despite all of these benefits, getting teachers up to a 3-second wait time turned out to be quite difficult. Waiting a little longer seemed simple but turned out to be difficult to learn: pauses of 1 second or less proved to be "almost immutable."[5]

It may seem that the last paragraph merely identifies a useful technique for improving the efficiency of learning, controlling student behavior, and improving test scores. Yet Rowe warned that "wait time . . . is just another technique if one does not understand why fostering more productive exchanges among us all is so important."[6] Her own interest in wait time was framed by an explicit desire to help students actively participate in reflective inquiry born of wonder rather than conformity. That is not quite the same vision as just manipulating time to more efficiently control student behavior, even if techniques for managing time are a necessary ingredient in fostering inquiry.[7] I wonder if the difference showed in her body language.

The ethical fabric of our pauses comes to the fore if we focus on one of Rowe's findings about how teachers changed. The variations in the length of teachers' pauses seemed to be associated with their expectations of students. When teachers saw a student as more able, they tended to offer a longer pause of hope. Their lower hopes for other students were reflected in shorter pauses. This seems like a direct inversion of Paul's New Testament vision of a body in which "the parts that we think are less honorable we treat with special honor" (1 Cor. 12:23). Training to lengthen teacher wait time enhanced respect and raised expectations for students who had previously been viewed as of limited ability. As teachers learned to wait longer, they heard more from those students to whom they had previously given less time to think. This effect "was particularly pronounced where minority students were concerned."[8]

Suddenly our questions become less mechanistic. The grounds for being interested in time expand to include questions of dignity and justice at the frayed edges of our capacity to approach all of our students with hope and honor.[9] Do our pauses of hope express our investment in all students' growth or just our own need to manage our performance and feel like we are moving along? Do our pauses of response honor the risk and potential represented by a student speaking up in class? How might the shape of our pauses enable some students while disadvantaging others? How might our prejudices show in our pauses? Such questions matter for ethical reasons, not just because of test scores, which is why "does it work?" is such an impoverished question if it is allowed to stand alone.

Consider some of the kinds of diversity in our classrooms. Students who are not native speakers of the language of instruction may need more time to process a teacher's question, formulate an answer, and gather the courage to speak. Short pauses of hope may intensify their existing disadvantage. Cultural differences may also come into play. Anglo-Americans tend to prefer seamless chatter, while Navajo politeness, for instance, places value on showing respect through extended silences.[10] Students formed in a culture that values longer conversational gaps may struggle to thrive in a classroom where quick-fire response is taken to be a mark of intelligence. The length of our pauses can become a kind of micro-climate for inclusion or exclusion.

In one of my education classes I sometimes teach intentionally poorly before asking students to unpack what they experienced. One behavior that I have used involves asking students rapid questions and being careful to break eye contact and move on a split second before a student has finished articulating their response. Maximum efficiency and minimum recognition is the message. When I asked students to reflect on what was happening, one summed up this teaching sequence succinctly: "you didn't care about us."[11] As I pointed out to my students, they cannot directly observe what is in my heart, but they can make inferences from my practices. The length of my pauses is one of those practices. It is relevant to the question of whether my teaching might count as an act of love.

Our small pauses are elusive. Even when we are paying attention, we are likely to be focused on what was just said, or what we will say next, or our fear of falling flat, rather than on the eloquence of the gaps. Yet attending to the pauses that pepper our classroom interactions can lure us into questions about justice, about hospitality to strangers, about inclusion and how to treat students as images of God. The big-sounding commitments may be narrated through small actions, and even through small silences.

Exercises

- Conversations about faith and learning have often focused mainly on whether Christian ideas and perspectives are taught or whether Christian heart attitudes are developed. How is this chapter different from those approaches?
- Focus on one hour in your teaching week when you will be leading class discussion. Pay attention to your own pauses and to what prompts the urge to break a silence quickly. What assumptions or anxieties seem to be driving your behavior?
- Ask a colleague to observe you in class with a focus on your pauses and on which students participate. Then compare your recollection of what happened with their perceptions.

PAUSING FOR BREATH

A few years ago I worked with a colleague, Marjorie Terpstra, to design and teach an online course about digital technology in the classroom. One of the topics we wanted to explore was how our use of digital devices tended to nudge us toward prioritizing speed, efficiency, and productivity over reflection, contemplation, and wonder. Our capacity to care well for people and other creatures, to listen carefully to God and neighbor, and to question our own overconfident interpretations is not well nurtured by relentless activity. Nurturing such capacities requires us to slow the scurrying squirrel of our mind sufficiently to see what is there and to hear voices that are not our own. Yet we seem to design and use our devices in ways that push hard toward seeing more things, getting more done, managing more information, and fostering the illusions of multitasking and omnipresence. Efficiency is a good thing in the right context, but it is not inevitably a good thing. I doubt that many of us want an efficient lover, and I don't think we should want an efficient prayer life. When efficiency replaces attentiveness, it can undermine learning as shortcuts take over from thought and engagement.[1] This is not a blanket argument for or against digital technology, just a reminder of our need to reflect on how our relationship to it relates to formation and wisdom.

One way of talking about wisdom in the biblical writings focuses on the capacity for delight. Proverbs 8 poetically describes the personified wisdom with which God shaped the world. The Christian church has found in this passage a glimpse of the Word that became flesh, without whom "not one thing came into being" (John 1:3) and in whom "all things hold together" (Col. 1:17). In this Proverbs poem, what does Wisdom get up to?

> I, wisdom, dwell together with prudence. . . .
> I walk in the way of righteousness,
> along the paths of justice,
> bestowing a rich inheritance on those who love me
> and making their treasuries full.
> The LORD brought me forth as the first of his works,
> before his deeds of old;
> I was formed long ages ago,
> at the very beginning, when the world came to be. . . .
> Then I was constantly at his side.
> I was filled with delight day after day,
> rejoicing always in his presence,
> rejoicing in his whole world
> and delighting in humankind. (Prov. 8:12, 20–23, 30–31)

You might pause here to seek out and read the whole chapter in Proverbs, perhaps more than once.

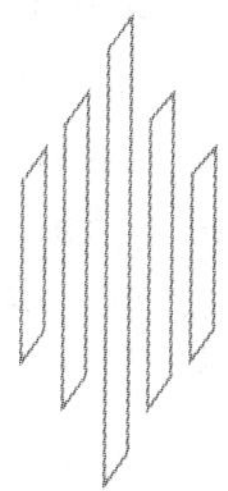

In Proverbs 8, we see Wisdom pursuing righteousness and justice, speaking faithfully, giving and receiving love, responding with generosity, and engaging in skillful crafts. This account of Wisdom's participation in creation culminates in a threefold delight. Wisdom is characterized by delight in God, delight in the created world, and delight in human beings. The very fabric of creation is being woven together in this passage, yet the focus is less on getting things done than on how skill fits together with love and justice in the context of joyful response. The passage continues:

Now then, my children, listen to me;
  blessed are those who keep my ways.
Listen to my instruction and be wise;
  do not disregard it.
Blessed are those who listen to me,
  watching daily at my doors,
  waiting at my doorway. (vv. 32–34)

Our capacity for delight is linked to our ability to watch, wait, listen, to receive what is good. If the ways of this Wisdom are to be ours, that will be reflected in our joy in God's presence, in a tree, a sunset, a text, or a molecule, in the touch of a friend, the ideas of a colleague, or the words of a wise stranger. Each of these becomes an echo of the wisdom at the root of the world.

In our empirical research on digital technology in schools, we found learners reporting that digital devices enabled them to delve deeper into topics and go beyond what the teacher knew. We also found learners describing how those same devices tempted them to use search capabilities to skim texts for quick answers instead of reading them, or to disengage in class and turn to distractions knowing that tasks would remain accessible later.[2] We found teachers appreciating the capacity of software to help them differentiate learning for the various needs of their students. We also heard teachers wrestling with the disappearance of the boundary between work and home (when is a teacher who is available by email not at work?) and intensifying pressure from students and parents for instant responses to messages. Technology promised getting more done quicker. Sometimes this seemed like a gain. Too often it also eroded learning and created stress.

We wanted the teachers in our online course on digital technology to think together about these tensions. Not without trepidation, we decided to risk three unusual assignments, each representing an invitation to pause for thought.[3]

First, we presented some of the reading assignments with an explicitly scripted focus on pacing and reflection. Here is a sample of our instructions from the second day:

> First, sit quietly for a full minute, listening to your breathing.
> Carefully navigate in *Digital Life Together* to chapter 2. . . .

Read just the quote at the beginning of the chapter.
Reread the quote, this time aloud or in a whisper.

- Perhaps you felt the same way when you wrote your response to the opening question for today.
- Perhaps you are one of those people who has "thought it through already."
- What questions arise in response to this quote?

As you slowly read the introduction to the chapter (the first two paragraphs), underline or highlight words and phrases that stand out to you.

This explicitly meditative framing provoked discussion among course participants as their routine study habits were interrupted. Some commented that they had seen this kind of thing in devotional contexts, but it would never have occurred to them as a classroom strategy. The change disrupted their expectations and made them adjust their approach to the assignment. We often think more about what we want students to read than about guiding them in how we want them to read. This degree of explicit guidance was something unexpected.

Snails and Trees

The next two assignments were designed to deepen the unease (I invite you to pause after each and try it for yourself before returning to continue with this chapter):

1. Go outside and find a tree. Any tree will do. Find a comfortable place to sit and observe the tree for five minutes. Think about all the different ways that a tree interacts with the world around it, with other creatures, with human beings. Notice its colors and movements. Think about its community of creatures (did you know that researchers found almost 950 beetle species—950 *species*, not 950 beetles—in fewer than twenty trees in Panama?).[4] Think about its history; is it older than you? What does it take from its environment? What does it give to its environment? Make time later to share what you noticed with someone else. As you observe, think of at least one question about trees that you could ask to deepen your understanding—something you don't know but could investigate online.

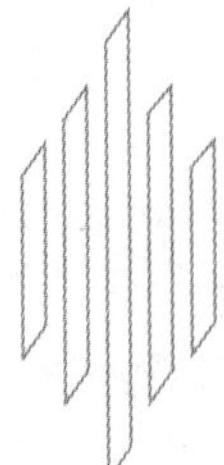

2. Porya Hatami is an electronic musician/sound artist in Iran. Pause here to reflect for a moment: What might you expect from an Iranian musician, and from a music video? The track "Snail" comes from his album titled *The Garden*. Watch the video for "Snail" attentively (https://vimeo.com/94817094) and reflect on what you see. After watching, consider: How difficult was it for you to slow down and attend to the small world of one creature for just 7.5 minutes? Did you gain any insight into the world of a snail? What feelings did you experience while watching this video? Disgust? Joy? Annoyance? Delight? Anger? How did the music/soundscape evoke the patient movement of a snail? What can you learn from observing a snail?

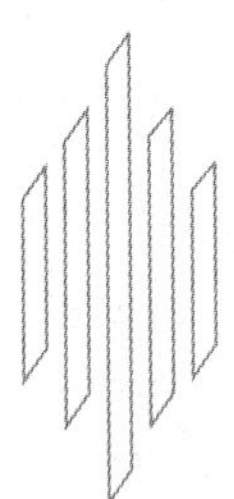

In these three assignments we asked participants to read slowly, to watch a tree for five minutes, and to watch a snail for seven minutes. These are simple tasks and small time investments. They are also a little unusual. As student responses made clear, they stepped well outside the expected script for an online course about technology and education.

In the discussion that ensued, it was striking how many students offered rueful reflections on how difficult these assignments were. Several confessed to experiencing an urge to skip ahead in the snail video, or a felt need to be getting something done, or an anxiety about laundry or cleaning they could have been doing. Some experienced anger at how the video forced them to wait. Along with these feelings came recognition that they said as much about us as about the video or the snail. Observing one creature for seven and a half minutes is not exactly moving to the monastery or signing up for an all-night vigil. Yet many of us have become almost incapable of slowing down and seeing a single creature for even this long without anxiety. What kind of teachers might that make us, we wondered. Teachers who can teach wisdom?

The word "permission" kept recurring. It was in the end refreshing, several teachers reflected, to be given permission to slow down, to look, to not be productive, to just enjoy what was there. One participant described taking her children outside their house for a conversation about the tree that had long stood in their yard. The conversation took an hour. She posted a photograph so the rest of us could see their tree. More than one teacher commented after the tree and snail activities, "I felt like I could breathe." It seems that many of us have a sense of needing explicit permission to slow down. What does that tell us about our educational culture, we wondered.

Talk of permission to breathe led naturally to discussion of the permissions that we in turn give to or withhold from our students through the rhythms of our teaching. There are larger cultural and institutional rhythms that are difficult for us to change, but we have some agency to shape time for our learners. How, we wondered, might we give permission to students and colleagues to stop equating productivity and learning? How might we foster a sense of beauty?

None of this was very efficient. It was not trying to be. The intent was to slow us, to interrupt, to focus us on questions about our ability to teach wisely rather than our ability to get more done. We were seeking learning tasks that might lay groundwork in learners for delight in the wider world, delight in other people, delight in their creator. The pauses were not time set aside from getting things done. They were one of the most essential parts of the learning.

Exercises

- Set this book aside and find a quiet place. Read Proverbs 8 slowly. Write a paragraph describing in your own words how the Bible's portrayal of wisdom might connect to how we design learning. Read Proverbs 8 again.
- How would you describe the pace of your own teaching? How do you think your students experience it? What kind of relationship to reality does it nurture? How could you best find out about student perceptions? Make some notes, then meet with a colleague and discuss your thoughts before investigating with students.
- Think of one learning activity that you could design for your classes that might enhance students' capacity for attentive delight in the things you are teaching. Then set it aside and design a second, different one.

PAUSING FOR CONNECTION

The church I attend holds an annual charity auction at which members offer goods and services and bid generously to raise money for Christian education. For several years, my wife and I offered a British tea party, with various baked goods and some history of tea drinking. (Did you know that in 1748 John Wesley published *Letter to a Friend, Concerning Tea*, advising that tea should be renounced as a poison?)[1] When my education students heard about it, they immediately wanted to know if they could have one too. So we concluded the semester with a tea party at my house, with much dressing up and plenty of clotted cream.

As the pile of scones diminished, I asked each student to name their most transformative moment of the semester. It was an intensive course, with an array of topics, projects, simulations, and activities. We had critiqued big ideas, taught in schools, designed curriculum, debated policy. With so much to choose from, surely there would be as many different responses as there were students. I was surprised when a fifth of the students chose the same moment, and I was surprised by the moment they chose.

Some hoped to teach in Christian schools, where classroom devotions might be expected, so I had intentionally modeled various ways of doing "devotions" that did not involve a perfunctory prayer and a paragraph read aloud from an inspirational book. One day, I entered class, sat down on the floor, and invited the students to join me, a move much less common at university than in kindergarten. After a silent pause, I asked each student to call out one word for how they were feeling.[2] They did so. I was silent again. Then I read a psalm aloud, slowly. After a final silence, I asked students to return to their seats, after which we continued with the rest of the day's agenda.

A fifth of my students named this as the most transformative moment of the semester. This, above so many elaborate interventions into which much more energy had been poured.

How Silence Speaks

Reflecting on silence as a form of hospitality, Jane Kelly Rodeheffer identifies some of the reasons why silence can be difficult for teachers:

> I like talking. This can be a virtue, enabling me to thrive in discussions. But it can also be a vice, causing me to crusade into every silence and confidently plant the flag of my opinion on the matter. This is especially dangerous as a teacher. I do well with those students who resemble my undergraduate self: eager to talk, willing to interrupt. But those students who need a bit more space, a bit more time—do I make my classroom hospitable to them? . . . I am fighting back. I am trying to talk less, to relinquish control over the direction and outcome of the conversation.[3]

The language of "fighting back" invites us to imagine silence not as absence of activity but as an intentional and intensive action, an intervention on behalf of others. My own students seem to have received the moments of intentional silence arranged around the psalm as an act of care and a contribution to learning, not simply as an absence of talk. I started wondering how many opportunities my students have to pause, to name how they are doing, to be heard, to sit in silence, to rest from leaning into the gale of activity and information and other voices. We tend to think of our words as the currency of the classroom. What are we saying by the pattern of our pauses?

Silence is not just absence. Of course it can be; there are moments when we simply have no thoughts worth sharing. But silence can also be reflective, receptive, contemplative, a pause to listen or to center ourselves. It can be focused, an intentional concentration on something that matters. It can be caring, holding back the comment that may discourage or undermine. It can be tense, filled with fraught anticipation of what is about to happen. It can be oppressive, generated by someone's intimidation, coercion, sarcasm, or domination. It can be prejudiced, amplifying favored voices while keeping others quiet. It can be insecure, avoiding speech for fear of being found foolish. It can be cowardly, failing to speak when others are harmed. In classrooms, as elsewhere, silence is not inherently good. It speaks with many voices.[4] Like words, silence can be approached with intentional awareness of what it is saying.

In the episode picked out by my students, I think silence functioned as a moment of care and respite amid a culture of hyperproductivity and exhaustion. Rebecca Konyndyk DeYoung describes a different kind of silence in a philosophy class on the seven deadly sins. While teaching about the concept of vainglory (the disordered desire to project an image that wins attention and approval), she assigned to her students (and to herself as a coparticipant) a week-long vow of silence.[5] Not literal silence, but a week of not talking about themselves. That meant:

> no commenting about your feelings, no offering your opinions or judgments, no wry witticisms or clever criticisms, no long-winded narratives about how your day went and what frustrated or elated you, no interrupting with "bigger and better" stories, no fishing for compliments, no calling or texting to share about what you're doing, no blogging about your opinions or favorite movies or annoying neighbors or pet peeves, no complaining. And perhaps hardest of all, no defending what you did, no preemptive spin to prevent others from getting the wrong impression of what you're doing, no rationalizing, no excuse-making. No nothing. Instead, be still. Listen. Let other people talk. Let your actions speak for themselves.[6]

Neither DeYoung nor her students anticipated quite how hard this would be. Through painful experience, they began to understand something that they "couldn't grasp through descriptions or reading instructions or observations of others' practice," namely, how much of their daily behavior was wrapped up in reputation management. Student journals suggested that the enforced pause functioned as a "moment of moral awakening, somewhat akin to the experience of someone pouring a bucket of ice water over their heads."[7] The point of the activity was not to gain mastery but rather to experience revelation of who we are and the chance to seek change. As smaller echoes of Sabbath, structured silences can function as small repentances, openings in our seamless tapestry of activity in which we might focus more clearly on God's work.

Silence as Connection

During research on how digital technology was reshaping the learning culture of Christian schools, my colleagues and I found teachers wondering how to resist the tendency of digital devices to reinforce an existing "culture of do, do, do, do, do."[8] One school had scheduled a weekly device-free hour focused on reflection and community building in mixed-age groups. It was an effort to regularly silence the barrage of digital information. The students we interviewed were very positive about this practice. They spoke of it as a relief of stress and as a chance to focus without the impulse to check for messages, though the community-building aspect was not going as well as hoped; "when we get together we just read," one student commented. Both students and teachers also reported seeing the supervising teachers sitting at the back of the device-free session working on laptops. One teacher summarized: "Kids are reading, teachers are on laptops." A colleague responded: "That's really sad."[9] The discrepancy was not lost on students.

When we pause together, the message is different from when we impose pauses on students without participating. The silence and psalm reading in my class would have spoken differently if I had remained standing and read from behind a podium, rather than sitting on the floor with my students, or if I had disengaged and checked email while the students sat in silence. Building the kind of shared practice that leads to spiritual growth calls for teachers to be implicated, walking the road, not just directing traffic. In the technology course discussed in the last chapter, the one in which we observed a tree and a snail and talked about permission to breathe, Paige Bokach, a science teacher, wrote:

> We might feel the pressure of so many standards, but our students don't have to. We can give permission to pause and appreciate beauty. I remember starting one class with a video of a salamander growing from one tiny cell to hundreds . . . watching how some were destined to become part of an eye, a finger, the heart. I felt guilty for taking the time (they had a test coming up!), but now I think that setting that time aside might be the whole point. What's the purpose of learning about living things if you never stop to think about the intricacy and creativity? Next time, I might ask students about the emotions

> they experienced—whether they were in awe, or just frustrated with the 8 minutes we took before moving on, or both. It might be good to honestly reflect on our own habits of thought . . . to grow to be more contemplative, observant, patient, curious, reverent, at peace. Frankly, I'll probably need it the most.[10]

When I read Paige's comments, I wonder again what kind of educational culture leaves a teacher feeling guilty for taking eight minutes to focus on the beauty of what is being learned. Her comments underline how pauses can serve beauty and wonder, but also how they challenge the teacher's capacity for disciplined engagement and call into question the larger institutional rhythms and expectations that we have created.

If we think of pauses as moments of connection and involvement, moments in which we become implicated rather than completing one more task, the results can be surprising. Recall the teacher mentioned in the last chapter, Pamela Tumwebaze, who responded to the tree assignment by taking her children into their back yard to watch the tree that had long stood there. Their contemplation turned into a long conversation. Several years later, she reflected back on how that moment helped them to connect with God and creation: "This was an enriching experience, for me and my children, because it was the first time we were appreciating the fauna and flora that surround our home. It was great to have a breath of fresh air. And that came after putting everything else away and paying attention to deep reflection, to slowing down. I still take outdoor walks with my boys and we still talk about how visible the hand of God is in the environment that surrounds us. . . . I have a better appreciation of Christian theology which is rich in depth and breadth."[11] As she allowed the structured pause to draw her in, it became more than a task to complete. It had a lasting influence on her relationship with her surroundings, her children, herself, and God.

Silence as Responsibility

Silence and pauses for reflection can mean many things, not all of them good. I think we should resist the tempting notion that silences are necessarily the spiritual part of learning, that the gaps are where God can work, that we make space for God when we stop teaching and step back out of the way. The idea that God only works in the gaps and silences suggests a part-time deity waiting in the wings, not the biblical creator, sustainer, and reconciler of all things. The idea that we can be Christian mainly in the pauses misses God's work in and through our activity. The point of the Sabbath, the paradigmatic pause, is not that God is absent the rest of the week or that God does no work in us on Tuesdays.

I am not suggesting that the silences are necessarily the spiritual moments. I am not suggesting that God starts working when we stop. Rather, I am suggesting that pausing, intentional silence, active holding back, is one of the responsible actions available to us as teachers. It is one of the ways in which we structure time. It can be a way to accuse or instill fear, or it can be a way to welcome, to show care and seek justice. It can point to beauty and truth. It can position us together as those who neither own nor control the world, and so need to receive, and it can help us reflect on how we can cooperate with God's work in us in our more obviously active moments. Through how we handle our pauses, we are implicitly teaching our students what we think about speech and silence, about control and restraint, about filling spaces or opening them, about grasping and receiving. Our pauses are one more way of confessing who we are and who we want our students to be.

Exercises

- Look back at the examples of silences and pauses in this chapter. Some, such as the psalm-reading episode, connect explicitly to Christian beliefs or devotional practices. Look at the ones that do not have such explicit connections to faith. In what ways might they also be plausible extensions of Christian interests?
- Think of an example from your own classroom of a good silence and a bad silence. How were they different? What shaped them? What was your role in shaping them?
- Think of one way to invite your students into an intentional silence or pause. Consider explicitly how it might implicate you, and how you can connect with your students in and through it. Ask a colleague and a student for feedback and suggestions.

PAUSING FOR HOSPITALITY

By David I. Smith and Joyce Nash Azaki[1]

DAVID: Some years ago, I was teaching an intensive graduate class in curriculum studies to a group that included students from multiple countries. The first significant written assignment came a few days into the course. I asked students to write about how their upbringing and identity were likely to bias their curriculum work. Which of their experiences and perspectives were most likely to nudge them toward creating learning resources that would be easier or harder for students from different backgrounds to access? Were there ways in which their own formational experiences might be a resource or make their curriculum work less hospitable?

One student in the class was Joyce Nash Azaki, a school leader from Nigeria with a vision for reshaping curriculum to better serve diverse learners. She wrote a thoughtful reflection on her own school experiences with large classes and a prescribed curriculum focused on memorization. I wrote to her recently to check my memory of what happened next against her perceptions. She agreed to tell her side of the story in her own words.

JOYCE: My beloved country, my motherland Nigeria, is a country located in West Africa with a current population of about 200,000,000 people. The nation has struggled to stand on her feet since independence from the British on October 1, 1960. The British had politically empowered groups who they believed were more friendly, and this contributed to underdevelopment, incompetent leadership, and socioeconomic strife. Nigeria, as with every other people group, has always had its own cultures and beliefs, as well as its traditional system of governance. The

British, on getting to Nigeria, fought the indigenous people and their native systems to impose British imperial rule. Those who vehemently opposed the occupying power were subjected to humiliation and ill treatment. Some were executed or dehumanized by the British, while others were favored and utilized. Social tensions arising from British colonial actions have contributed to underdevelopment and socioeconomic strife. Incompetent leadership has contributed its own problems. Due to my own experiences and position in Nigerian culture, I associated Britain strongly with past colonial violence.

DAVID: As I read Joyce's reflections, I was in new territory. My knowledge of Nigerian history was close to zero. I was educated in British schools and received a solid dose of history classes, but I do not recall being taught about this facet of Britain's involvement in the wider world, or much about the history of African countries in general. But this was not a history class. It was when Joyce went on to describe how her sense of history affected her ability to participate in my class that I began to panic.

JOYCE: EDUC 522 was a class I looked forward to, especially since it was a curriculum course, and I would always sit and try to listen to Professor Smith as he lectured, but as hard as I tried, I would always hear his British accent bringing back horrible images of British colonial history in Nigeria. As much as I was ostensibly listening to his lecture, deep in my thoughts the portrait of a colonial past was what was standing before me. My perception, and not what he was teaching, dominated what I was hearing and seeing. In essence, what I was supposed to be learning from him was not happening.

His commanding presence in the class as a professor succeeded in reminding me of the British colonial exploitation and how it contributed to present injustices, political problems, and inequalities. Ethnic tensions fueled by the British "divide and rule" political strategy contributed to postindependence challenges in Nigeria. Because of my own relationship to this history, I resented the British professor standing before me.

DAVID: I confess that in the first moment my reaction was not admiration for the courage and relevance of Joyce's comments. At first, all I could hear was rejection. I was a bad teacher and a bad person. I was too ignorant of the world of my students to serve their needs well. There was also some self-pity and resentment in the mix. I had never even been to Nigeria. I was not the one who committed crimes of which I knew nothing. It was not fair to bundle me together with folk with whom I had a tenuous connection beyond my genes and my accent. It was not my fault, and I was being stereotyped. There was a lot of insecurity too. How could I even continue teaching the class if this is what my voice sounds like to this student, and if these are the perceptions my presence is evoking for her?

I think my outward response was polite, but like Joyce, I had to work to process my inward reactions. Pausing to think the matter through and move out from the knot of my own vulnerability, I began to wonder what my options were. I could start researching Nigerian history to see if I could find loopholes in Joyce's account, since the social tensions it mentioned implied that there would be other versions of the story. I could insist that she is in America now and needs to buckle down to learning. I could protest my personal innocence and ask to be treated based on my individual virtues and defects. But pausing gave me prayerful space to wonder what story my response might tell about my own relationship to power, to hospitality, to learning. Responding in a manner that appeared to confirm the stereotype did not seem a promising path toward changing it. My responses to difficult moments with students are, like it or not, part of what I teach.

When we next met, I asked Joyce if she would be willing to lead the class for a short time at the beginning of our session on Monday morning. Knowing her gifts and strength of personality, I thought it could work. I suggested that because the whole class was working toward an understanding of how identity can shape teaching and learning and affect access to curriculum, it could be very helpful for everyone to hear Joyce's reflections on how her perspectives were affecting her learning. We would not be off topic. I asked her to explain to the class how her understanding of the British role in Nigeria had impacted her ability to learn in a curriculum class in Michigan led by a British person. I asked whether she was comfortable with the idea. She agreed, and I gave the opening minutes of the class session over to her.

JOYCE: Now, I wasn't sure it was a good idea that Prof. Smith asked me to share my thoughts with the larger group, but what I am certain of is that I remember a few of my colleagues who sat close to me whispering admonitions that would have discouraged me when I started to speak. The atmosphere became tense; I guess some thought I was directly attacking the professor, but I was just expressing myself in relation to my awareness of what British people had done in Nigeria and how this class came across to me as meeting with the colonialist.

DAVID: I remember consciously reflecting on where I should be while Joyce led the group. If I stood hovering to one side, I would not be yielding the floor. Joyce's voice would be visibly curated and framed by mine. I wanted to model a humility that showed a willingness to yield the center and make space for a perspective that did not flatter me so that we could learn from it. The room where we met had a low ledge running around the walls, about a foot from the floor. I went to a corner and sat on it until Joyce had finished her story. I was conscious that where I positioned myself was also curriculum.

JOYCE: One good thing that sharing with the larger group did for me was to afford me opportunity to ventilate vestiges of British colonization in Nigeria, which sincerely lightened the burden I have carried over the years concerning the impact of the British on my people. That British accent in the classroom was until now for me a symbol of pain and injustice. Nevertheless, talking about it and having a class discussion around it without obstruction made me see a Briton who was ready to give me the opportunity to let others at least hear my story and perspective on how my roots and identity were shaping and contributing to my learning, notwithstanding whether my history and related feelings and pains were the subject of discussion or not. I was and am thankful for this opportunity as my learning for the rest of the semester was never the same again.

DAVID: I was aware of risks. My lack of relevant background knowledge meant that I could do little to expand on what students heard about Nigeria, even if other accounts might complicate the picture; the topic firmly removed me from the position of expertise. But the center of attention was on understanding the learning process, not Nigerian history. I had no guarantee that this experiment would change anything. But the purpose was not to fix everything; it was merely to create an opportunity for Joyce to be heard and for the rest of us to think with her about how her history, experiences, and perceptions impacted teaching and learning. There is no guarantee that it would go the same way on another occasion, or with a different person, or in a different class. This is a story, not a recipe.

My own interest here is in how my faith interacts with my teaching decisions. Pausing to reflect and to pray interrupts at least two processes that are otherwise at risk of determining most of what I do as a teacher. One is the persistent patter of my instinctive thoughts and feelings. Though I trust that some healthy formation has happened over the years, and I have more capacity for sober reflection than when I started, my first reactions and responses do not always arise from the ground of my faith or my best virtues. The other is the rushing routine of habitual teacher behaviors: the way we always do things, the way I did it last week, and the need to get to the next task. Unless I actively choose to pause, what I do next is likely to echo the pattern of what is always done, for good or ill. Pausing lets me question the obvious options. It creates a little space to ask myself questions. What does it mean for *this* moment that *this* student is made in God's image? What might it look like in teaching terms to not "lord it over one another," or to "consider others better than yourselves" (Matt. 18:1–4; Phil. 2:3–11)? What might count as humility, as care, as justice? How might all of this flow together with all my other teaching and learning goals?

The pause does not make space for God, who is present in everyday words and actions as much as in thoughtful silences. The pause makes space for me to take God and the others in the room into account. The pause does not guarantee that I will choose wisely. Yet in this instance, it was with gratitude and wonder that I learned from Joyce later in the course that our interaction had cleared the air for her, that she had been able to learn more easily for the rest of the course.

JOYCE: I did not imagine that this one opportunity of letting my voice be heard in a class would mean this much to my learning and thinking as an educator, but it did in many ways.

Coming from a system of education where the professor and teachers know it all, my experience in EDUC 522 taught me that as an educator I will need to learn about my individual students in order to make a difference in their learning. Humility from my professor is one thing that I learned from the class; I learned the need to pay attention to what my students might be saying or thinking by listening more to my students and by giving them opportunity to express themselves. Hence, as a teacher, even when I might feel I am in charge, listening will only help me be a better educator and not an educational dictator/prescriber.

Creating a learning environment where every learner can be free to share without being judged or ridiculed is a lesson I cannot forget. I am striving to be that educator whose learners will see schools as the safest place they can flourish irrespective of where they are coming from or what they think about themselves.

Exercises

- Articulate in your own words one way in which Christian convictions were at work in this exchange. Then set that aside and look for a second way.
- Find a quiet place to think. Reflect prayerfully on those moments when you feel most threatened or disoriented as a teacher, and what instinctive reactions arise for you in those moments. What are your strategies for moving from those instinctive reactions to an intentional response grounded in hope and love? Take some time out to share your strategies with a colleague and ask about theirs.
- Identify a student to whom you might need to listen more carefully. Think of a nonthreatening way to hear from them about how they are experiencing your class. Then set aside time to reflect on how you might respond.

REPEATING

RHYTHMS OF IMAGINATION

As a semester progresses, patterns emerge. Some topics and allusions recur. Certain gestures and emphases return at regular intervals. We review, we remind, we repeat, and in the pattern of our repetitions there are clues as to what story we are trying to tell.

In the preface to a recent book on theological education, Elizabeth Conde-Frazier describes some of the repetitions she experienced during her childhood as a member of a Latin@ church in New York.[1] In her church, children were drawn into ministry early as ushers, visitors of the sick, assistants with communion, deacons, and Sunday school helpers. They were actively mentored by adults who had gifts in these areas and through summer workshops. Annual festivals were marked by consuming food from various regions and openly celebrating cultural diversity in the congregation. Sunday school leaders were required to attend a midweek Bible study at which the pastor pushed them to articulate scriptural grounds for any points they wanted to make but did not dictate what points should be made. That combination of normativity and freedom created "space for theological thinking with the capacity to hold on to a diversity of views."[2] (I hope that the present book reflects a similar spirit.) In sermons, the same pastor "always asked where a particular view came from," so that "we learned to identify contexts with theological and historical differences."[3] When taking questions, "he made it clear that it was fine not to have answers to the mystery of God's love for all the world."[4]

Everything Conde-Frazier describes here is a repeating pattern, not a onetime intervention. It is clear from her description that these patterns, repeated over time in the weekly and annual renewal of community life, were deeply formative for her own approach to Christian ministry. These were not the numbing repetitions of a mechanical drill session, nor were they the kind of learning that happens through explanatory speeches. They were recurring nudges, intentional rhythms, a process of learning carried in the iterative contours of shared behaviors.

I did not grow up with any such patterns of church life. I experienced little direct contact with churches before arriving at university as an argumentative atheist. I had been to a handful of church services. I attended a youth organization whose programming included some Christian teaching, but I was mostly interested in the social activities. I experienced compulsory religious education in school that included coverage of Christianity. Some foundations were no doubt laid.

Yet when my world broke open and I became part of a student Christian group, it was with a sense of learning from a fresh start what being Christian entailed. I launched into a new cadence of prayer and Bible study meetings, mission trips and conferences, Christian books, Christian music, and sermon recordings. As the end of my studies neared, I committed to praying, fasting, and seeking counsel in an effort to discern how I should invest my adult life. A clear conviction formed in me: I should become a teacher.

I was relieved to find an answer, but also a little disappointed and disoriented.

As I processed that reaction, I gradually realized that the patterns of practice that had cradled my own brief journey as a new Christian had created hurdles for my imagination. They were not as nourishing for my future calling as those experienced by Elizabeth Conde-Frazier apparently were for hers.

I gradually realized I had internalized an implicit theology of vocation that went something like this. Anyone fully committed to God would be called to be a missionary, preferably in a country without modern conveniences so that the effort would be visibly heroic. Those slightly less earnest could be pastors (still preaching the gospel, but on home territory and with an income) or youth pastors (still "ministry" but with more pop culture). Next came helping professions: nursing, teaching, social work. Faint embers of faith or outright worldliness might lead to careers in business, politics, or rock music. I had been taught that what kept Christians from the mission field was their unwillingness to say yes to God. I thought I had been sincere in asking God to call me to whatever he wanted. The answer seemed to ask for less than I had been willing to give.

Implicit Learning

This tension rumbled around at the back of my mind for a few years. As I read and learned more and moved into new contexts, I gradually became convinced that this picture of a hierarchy of callings was mostly false. Attending more closely to passages such as Colossians 1 shifted my perception of what the gospel might entail. In Colossians 1, Paul presents Christ as the agent of both creation (vv. 15–17) and reconciliation (vv. 18–20), and as he brings the two together, with Christ at the heart of both, he uses parallel phrases to describe each:

> The Son is the image of the invisible God, the **firstborn** over all creation. For in him **all things** were created: **things in heaven and on earth**, visible and invisible, whether thrones or powers or rulers or authorities; **all things** have been created through him and for him. He is before **all things**, and in him **all things** hold together.
>
> And he is the head of the body, the church; he is the beginning and the **firstborn** from among the dead, so that in **everything** he might have the supremacy. For God was pleased to have all his fullness dwell in him, and through him to reconcile to himself **all things**, whether **things on earth or things in heaven**, by making peace through his blood, shed on the cross.

As many things as are created are reconciled. All things. It does not sound as if the point is to elevate a few religious activities by downplaying the importance of everything else. The challenge seems more like figuring out how reconciliation touches everything. I found a commentary in which N. T. Wright put it this way:

> There is no sphere of existence over which Jesus is not sovereign, in virtue of his role both in creation (1:16–17) and in reconcilia-

> tion (1:18–20). There can be no dualistic division between some areas which he rules and others which he does not. . . . The logic of this message requires that those who announce it should be seeking to bring Christ's Lordship to bear on every area of human and worldly existence. Christians must work to help create conditions in which human beings, and the whole created world, can live as God always intended.[5]

This vision of good news made a lot more space for the possibility that being a teacher was a meaningful calling, one that could stretch my faith as far as it would go. I slowly made peace with the idea that as I taught French and German to teenagers, I was not just biding my time until I could afford to go to seminary.

What I started to wonder was how I had learned such a skewed view of vocation in the first place. I do not remember anyone standing up and saying, in so many words, "It's best to be a missionary, or you could make do with being a pastor, but you might want to avoid business and politics." Nevertheless, in my few years as a Christian, I had internalized something very like that picture. If I did not learn it through direct, verbal instruction, how did I learn it?

I think I learned it in large measure through repeating rhythms, recurring patterns of representation, emphasis, and absence. I can identify a few of them.

There were regular Christian meetings at which pastors and missionaries were given a raised podium with chairs facing it in rows and asked to talk about their work. Those who worked in business or the arts were less likely to occupy the same position of symbolic prominence. There were special meetings for those considering the mission field but not for would-be teachers. Some callings, it seemed, were worthy of focal attention and visible distinction; others, less so.

At prayer meetings, we prayed for missionaries and pastors, for evangelism, and for personal needs. I do not recall prayer for the work of scientists, construction workers, translators, therapists. Some work, it seemed, was worth talking to God about, other kinds were not, conveying the impression that God was less keen to hear about them.

The biographies in my local Christian bookstore (I devoured many) were about pastors, missionaries, and evangelists. Sermon illustrations followed suit. At one point I bought two old books in a used bookstore, each containing assorted short biographies of worthy past Christians. One focused on evangelists and church leaders. Through my time spent in Christian circles, I had already heard of two-thirds of them. The other focused on Christians who had worked to resist slavery, make provision for the poor, found schools, and more. I had heard of three of them.[6] Some stories, it seemed, were worth repeatedly retelling; others could be quietly forgotten.

The logic of sacrifice in the stories I read and heard always seemed to involve people who abandoned promising careers in, say, law or medicine to become preachers or make missionary journeys to exotic overseas locations. I did not hear stories about those who leave missionary work or otherwise sacrifice to take up other forms of service.

There were, of course, direct words, stirring calls to consider missions and the like, but I suspect that these were at the very least reinforced by such repeating patterns of practice. My imagination was formed by the things that always happened and never happened when faith was in focus. When I did hear God call me to significant work, I struggled to receive what I heard because it did not fit the template formed in my imagination by the habitual moves of the Christian community of which I was a part.

For good or ill, our students learn how faith fits into the world not just from our explanations but also from our gestures, rhythms, and silences. They learn from the things we habitually connect and the things we leave detached. They learn from the contexts that seem to trigger faith talk and the ones that don't. They learn from what we consider worth praying for and whom we consider worthy of an audience. They learn from the selection of stories that we seem to regard as noble, from the examples we keep in circulation, and from the absence of the ones we don't mention. Our repetitions lay down a rhythm that tempts learners toward particular dance steps. The dance can be freeing, as for Elizabeth Conde-Frazier, or constricting, as in my own experience. The result is not an iron cage; as I wrestled with my own sense of calling, I soon began to resist the patterns that had begun to shape me. But I do wonder whether it had to be that hard.

Exercises

- What repeating behaviors in church settings have shaped your perceptions of what it means to be Christian? What implicit messages do these repetitions carry? How do they affect your assumptions about what it means to be Christian in a classroom?
- How might a student's faith formation affect their approach to learning? And how might our teaching practices affect a student's faith formation? Give one concrete example of each process.
- Reflect on one kind of repetition within your school culture, such as the pattern of what is publicly celebrated, what stories are shared, who gets to speak, how learning is justified to students, or how prayer is performed in public. Write a paragraph describing it in concrete detail. How do you think students are being formed by the pattern? Should the pattern be punctured or reshaped? Share your notes on these questions with a colleague and a student for feedback.

RHYTHMS OF SEEING

Art historian Joanna Ziegler describes a learning assignment that strikes me as unusually courageous.[1] It goes like this.

In the first week of the semester, Ziegler asks her students to visit the nearby art museum. Students are given a choice of three artists and must select a painting by one of them. They are told not to consult any outside reading or the explanation on the museum wall, but simply to observe the painting and then write an essay of no more than five typed pages about what they see and turn it in. Beyond some initial student anxiety about whether they would find anything to write, this is not too unsettling.

Seeing Again . . . and Again

It is after the first week that things take an unexpected turn. In the second week of the semester, and in every subsequent week, Ziegler asks her students to repeat the assignment. Take the same means of transportation, go at the same time in the week, enter the museum through the same door, sit in the same spot, look at the same painting, and rewrite the same essay.

Ziegler's students were not immediately thrilled. As she points out, we expect extended repetition in some areas of learning. Repeating physical exercises, practicing a piece of music, or drilling vocabulary fit tidily into our imagination. Multiple drafts of a single essay are not unusual. But repeating the same observations and the same writing assignment multiple times breaks the expected pattern. (Ironically, the expected pattern feels normal because of our repeated experience of being asked to express ideas and opinions about a text or artifact after engaging with it only once or twice.)

Ziegler frames her departure from the norm by quoting from an essay on Benedictine spirituality. It emphasizes that "the disciple's goal is to hear keenly and sensitively that Word of God which is not only message but event and encounter." Approaching this goal entails learning to "listen closely, with every fiber of our being."[2] Learning to listen attentively for God's voice requires nurturing a capacity to stop spiraling around self-centered preoccupations and to still our inner chorus. It is not something we take to naturally, but rather a discipline to be learned. Might learning art history be an activity that can contribute something to fostering an attentive self?

In the early going, Ziegler's students were openly negative about the required repetition. Such initial negativity is not necessarily a sign that a course change is needed. It may instead be evidence that we need sustained help in submitting to structures that begin to expose our addiction to self. This is where teachers can help us, gently yet insistently.[3] In time, Ziegler's students came to value the opportunity to reflect and the stability of this one routine in their busy and complex weeks. Their writing revealed significant changes over time:

> The essays transformed tangibly from personalized, almost narcissistic, responses to descriptions firmly grounded in the picture. Descriptions evolved from being fraught with willful interpretation, indeed selfishness (students actually expressed hostility at being made to go to the Museum once a week), to revealing some truth about the painting on its own terms. . . . Through repeated, habitual, and direct experience (not working from slides or photographs but confronting the real work of art), students were transformed from superficial spectators, dependent on written texts for their knowledge, into skilled, disciplined beholders with a genuine claim to a deep and intimate knowledge of a single work of art—and they knew it.[4]

The repeating activity, "resisted at first but embraced by the end," offered an invitation to become more skilled at seeing and interpreting art.[5] Along with this came an opportunity to grow in the ability to resist preoccupation with self and convenience and to develop a capacity for contemplation.

We should be careful about swift equivalences here. Attending well to a work of art is not the same thing as listening to God. Getting better at interpreting a painting is not salvation from self; it could instead feed our pride. But could it help develop capacities that are of value to those who set store by the ability to listen for God's voice? If we attach importance to the capacity to read Scripture deeply and repeatedly, to give ourselves to prayerful contemplation, to become aware of our self-centered focus, and to listen for voices outside our own concerns, then it seems we ought to value practices that slow us down and poke uncomfortably at our self-preoccupation. Might those same capacities be left undeveloped, or even undermined, by a drive for efficient coverage of material? The argument here is not so much "this will achieve that" (art history as a substitute for prayer) as "those who value this ought to also value that."[6]

Once we think in these terms, the canvas widens beyond art history. A science teacher in a PreK-12 Christian school system described a similar assignment focused on students' ability to pay attention to creation. Students were asked to choose a small and accessible area of land and visit it at regular intervals, attending to how it changed, the creatures that could be observed, the sounds, smells, and colors. As the teacher recounted, the results spilled over beyond the bounds of science learning:

> Students can choose a natural spot of land anywhere that's easy access for them, and then they track seasonal change from when school starts in August through December. They create a blog where they're . . . basically documenting, and they run one experimental design that they design, and plan, and carry out themselves. They're amazing, some of your photographers, some of your writers, oh my word. . . . I had a student come to me initially and say, "can I combine this blog with a project I'm doing for creative writing?" and I said, "yes!" One of those moments of, "that's awesome!" So I have more and more students who are starting to combine them with something they are doing in Spanish, and something they are doing in creative writing. It's really cool. I had a student make a book . . . [about] her grandfather's land. She made a book of all her photos for him for Christmas. Then she brought me the pictures in, of when she gave it to him, and I was bawling . . . ah! It was amazing.[7]

It seems that when students began from attentiveness to creation, they soon discovered connections among their various school subjects, which became less like sealed compartments and more like different forms of access to a world with its own integrity. They discovered that paying close attention to a piece of land might also mean paying attention to what it means for the people connected with it. Attentiveness led to acts of care. It seems likely that the teacher's framing of the task and support for student reflection played a large role in sustaining this trajectory.

Missy Bryan, a professor who teaches occupational therapy at a Christian university, similarly picked up on the connections between repetition, attentiveness, and care as she described to me a case study assignment from one of her classes. She wrote:

> I find that students are so used to being able to find massive amounts of quick information and surface knowledge, that they have difficulty truly slowing down and deeply engaging in a single assignment or topic. To combat this, I have students explore a series of topics using a single case study. They follow the same client along a continuum of care. They often question why we are using the same case over and over, but it is because I want them to know their client deeply, so that they are more effective in understanding and meeting his or her needs.[8]

Repetition here is serving love of neighbor. Once again, the chain of inference starts from the instructor valuing attentive care for others and the ability to give of oneself. Those values then inform learning structures that build capacity to attend closely and repeatedly and create some disruption to the routine of managing information. The structure of the task communicates to students that the goal is not just to get through the various kinds of material but to learn to give their attention to the people they are preparing to serve.

What Repetition Says

My interest here is primarily in what is at stake in the teacher's choices. Repetition communicates what we value in the world that we study. This particular thing, we are saying, is worth returning to. Repetition communicates an implicit story about learning. Your learning, we are saying, involves your dispositions and your character, not just your cleverness and productivity. Repetition also suggests a vision of the needs of students. You will grow, we are saying, if you begin to become less like this and more like that.

The examples described above communicate in all three of these ways. In each one, asking for repeated attention to a single part of creation (a painting, a place, a person) communicates that this was valued by the teacher and worthy of the student's focus. Each repetition implied that what is studied has a complex integrity that cannot be exhausted or mastered in a single exposure and summary. We must return to see what we missed, to further appreciate what we saw or heard. The invitation to reinvest time suggests that here is something worthy of intentionally renewed engagement. By insisting on repetition, we point a nonverbal finger at some facet of creation and say, "attend here; this matters at a level deeper than immediate utility." What among the things that we ask students to study matters enough to merit this kind of engagement?

The second message, a story about learning, is already implicit in the first. What do we communicate to students if the only things repeated with any intensity are low-level skills, or reminders not to cheat, or nagging about deadlines, or acts of grading? What do students learn about repetition if it is only applied to drills and mechanical tasks? What do we communicate about learning if texts are only read once before inviting a judgment, or if breadth of coverage always trumps depth of engagement, or if lingering over and returning to the beauty of something studied is an infrequent luxury? Our uses of repetition say something about the kind of learning we think students should experience.

By now the third message is in plain sight. Repetition tells a story about the capacities we suspect students might lack and the capacities they most need to develop. The teacher who is convinced, say, that poor spelling is a key student failing is likely to push repeated engagement with spelling skills. By the same token, when an art teacher talks of overcoming student selfishness and developing intimate knowledge, when a science teacher encourages widening connections and is most amazed by the honoring of a grandfather, when a professor of occupational therapy asks students to know a client deeply for the sake of the client's needs, each is communicating their vision of what students can do, what failings need to be targeted, and how humans should grow. A key means by which they communicate this is repetition. Intentional, thoughtful repetition expresses our beliefs about what it means for humans to live well and invites students to test-drive those beliefs.

Not everything is in the end worthy of repeated engagement. Not every kind of repetition moves us forward. Not every act of attentiveness is the same thing as prayerful contemplation. Yet if repetition can be a signal of what is worthwhile, a way to deepen learning, and a discovery of how we need to change, then it is worth attending carefully to our repetitions. What if not just our ability to spell and calculate but also our ability to respond to the world with loving attention were the focus of intentionally repeated engagement? Overrepetition of words can diminish their value. But educators who value delight in creation, care taken with the work of others' hands, and love of neighbor have good reason to repeat themselves in other idioms.

Exercises

- Repeating things is not necessarily a Christian move. Based on this chapter, under what circumstances do you think using repetition can become something tethered to Christian convictions? What kinds of repetition might not have the same connection?
- Identify one specific way you want your learners to grow, one that is rooted in your beliefs about what is true and good and beautiful. If you have them, you could usefully refer back to your thoughts in response to the exercises on page 44. Make notes on how you could communicate this goal through repetition—not just by repeatedly telling students about it but through repeating learning experiences. Share your ideas with a colleague and a student for feedback.

RHYTHMS OF READING

Reading is a frequent practice in most kinds of courses, yet after the earliest years of schooling we often take it for granted. Students continue to receive instruction in effective writing all the way up to university-level education, yet we tend to talk about reading as something we learned to do at a very young age. Assignments for older students often name only what is to be read, assuming that students know how to read and that the generic ability to decode text will suffice.[1]

In a German literature course that I used to teach, I worked at creating a pattern of learning practices focused on the idea of charitable reading.[2] We spent the semester increasing our understanding of modern German literature, and at the same time we examined our own reading practices through the lens of charity, justice, humility, and patience (see ASSIGNING). We explicitly worked on our ability to approach the words of others with attentiveness, to avoid judging too quickly, to be careful with our praise and criticism, to reread fruitfully, to be alert for what our own biases and preoccupations might have helped us miss, and to treat a piece of writing as the work of a neighbor's hands. Student feedback across several iterations of the course suggested that it was an impactful experience. Repetition played a significant role in the course design.

The kind of repetition in play here was the repetition of reengagement, returning to a text or an idea with eyes wide open, willing to think again and to see what more we had to learn. It was a kind of repetition that aimed to push us past first impressions and convenient closure. The point was not just to reread something for reinforcement, to help us remember information, but to revisit texts to see where our previous reading fell short. The discipline of intentional return was meant to push back against the tendency to treat texts as tasks that we can check off and discard, reminding us weekly that we were seeking wisdom rather than productivity. In my experience, many students, well trained to extract information from a text and then move on, need structured help to engage well with a text from which they have already gleaned the main points.

One of our repetitions simply involved reading and discussing the same story more than once. There was an explicit focus on noticing what we had missed instead of always focusing on quick mastery.[3] Another form of repetition, which I will unpack a little here, involved a recurring weekly pattern of encounters with very short texts that ran alongside the main content of the course. They served as a kind of accompanying commentary on what we were doing as we worked through the main course texts.

Tuning In

These short texts were of two kinds. First, there was a weekly poem by the same poet (I chose Hans Magnus Enzensberger). Students were to read the poem by Monday, submit a translation by Wednesday, and submit a journal reflection by Friday. I replied by email to students' translations and journals, giving feedback but no grade. This created a running weekly dialogue that circled around our efforts to get better at grasping Enzensberger's sometimes elusive tone and challenging ideas. As the semester unfolded, I watched students' responses become more complex, informed, and assured. They began to comment on what a certain line probably did not mean because "Enzensberger would not be likely to say that," a judgment that they had rarely been in a position to make in more conventional survey courses. They gradually gained a sense of the turns Enzensberger was likely to take, the things that seemed to drive him to criticism or wonder.

As they got to know Enzensberger, they gradually tuned in to what I was looking for in their journals. I wanted both attentiveness to the text and a willingness to give personal space to its ideas. If the poem said incisive things about consumerism, or hope, or apathy, then just describing the details of the rhyme scheme seemed a poor testimony to our ability to listen to its voice. Yet leaping into our own feelings about the topic with little evidence of noticing the details of Enzensberger's text would equally miss the mark. In the early weeks, students often veered to one pole or the other, offering formal summaries or impressionistic anecdotes. As I responded to each journal, I suggested adjustments for the next time. "That's an interesting thought—can you tie it for me to anything Enzensberger did with words in line 3?" "You're right, that word appears a lot, but why?" Gradually, week by week, students tuned in to what I was after. The dialogue became richer. The journals provided formative assessment that helped guide my teaching. They also helped me see the value of repeating structures in which students and instructor can work gradually and imperfectly toward a complex skill before we start thinking about grades.

Attempts to say what matters are easily trumped by the question of what is on the test. At the end of my literature course I experimented with several forms of final assessment. The one that seemed to resonate the most with my students involved asking them to find a poem by Enzensberger that we had not read and discussed in class and write a reflective commentary on it. I reminded students that they had spent thirteen weeks doing this, gradually learning to catch Enzensberger's voice, to spot his favorite moves, to listen to the worries and joys embodied in his poetry, to develop an ear for what he might say and relate it to their lives. Given the modest number of people in the United States who read poems in German by Hans Magnus Enzensberger, I told them there was a reasonable chance that they were now among the best interpreters of his poetry in the nation. I expressed my hope (often fulfilled) that I would learn things from each of their commentaries. After thirteen ungraded iterations, this final one would be graded. One student lingered after class to tell me that this was the first time they had looked forward to a final assessment. Usually, they said, it felt as if their teachers were trying to catch them out on the things they forgot or misunderstood. This time it felt as if their teacher wanted them to show what they could do now.

Seeking Guides

The second kind of short text was a biweekly paragraph drawn from the rich tradition of Christian reflection on reading as an act of love. Responding to these became part of that week's journal activity. They served as a mirror held up to our own reading practices. They provided a language with which to comment on how we were doing. They functioned as what Etienne Wenger calls an "infrastructure of imagination," a kind of scaffolding to help us to imagine what we were doing in the light of past Christian reflection.[4]

An example may make it easier to imagine this. One of the texts was a paragraph from Mikhail Bakhtin:

> The valued manifoldness of Being as human . . . can present itself only to loving contemplation. . . . Lovelessness, indifference, will never be able to generate sufficient attention to slow down and linger intently over an object, to hold and sculpt every detail and particular in it, however minute . . . an indifferent or hostile reaction . . . always . . . impoverishes and decomposes its object.[5]

The main ideas are quite plainly stated, but that opening phrase made us work, and that was good for our conversation. I take Bakhtin to be saying, at least in part, that understanding the human world is hard for more than one reason. Humans have many layers; they are complex. But on top of that, neither we nor the humans we seek to understand are detached and objective. Human affairs are shot through with our values, and when I try to understand others and their products, I have to reckon with both the values shaping them and the values shaping how I hear them (and then their reaction to how I hear them, and so on). Our best chance at sustaining enough attention to wade through all of this and hear well is to learn loving contemplation. If we cannot love, we caricature before we hear, reducing others to general categories or a few cherry-picked details. Only love will take the time to let others appear to us in their wholeness.

Bakhtin's thoughts resonated with the core themes of the course and gave us some questions to explore. Is he right that our ability to approach a text with love affects our chances of reading it well? Does "loving" mean we have to like the text or agree with it, or does Bakhtin have something else in mind here? What other kinds of love are there? What does it mean to love people we dislike or disagree with?

As we discussed this paragraph, Bakhtin's metaphor of sculpting became a resource. We talked about sculptors looking at their model, then back at the medium, then back at the model, then back at the medium, making an adjustment here, a correction there. Was our reading like that, going back and forth between the text and our interpretation to see if we had created a false representation? Or were we hoping for something more like an instant digital snapshot on a tourist trip? As time passed I heard students asking one another at the start of class whether they had managed to sculpt this week's poem.

Other weeks brought other voices. I wanted to show that we were not the first to think about charitable reading. I wonder what might have been gained by engaging repeatedly with a single paragraph such as Bakhtin's, perhaps once a month across the semester, coming back to it and asking whether we had learned anything from it since last time. I have begun to play with this possibility in other courses, sometimes choosing a quotation that captures a challenging thought at the heart of our inquiry and asking students to reflect on it at the beginning, partway through, and again at the end. Sometimes students quote such texts back to me in conversation later. Perhaps an eloquent articulation of what we are trying to learn would be a good candidate to be inscribed on our memory.

I don't think this kind of thing is unique to the literature classroom. What kind of paragraph might fruitfully join teacher and students in shared, repeated meditation on some of the deep goods involved in appreciating mathematics, understanding paintings, or pursuing scientific investigation? What kind of paragraph might evoke the beauty and complexity of our subject area while speaking with the accents of faith? What version would work for elementary school students, for graduate students? Might repeatedly weaving such a paragraph into class reflection be more eloquent in the long run than a single assignment or a devotional thought at the start of class?

Mindless repetition has diminishing returns; we filter out the sound of traffic after a while, and we can do the same to other meaninglessly repeated stimuli. Hectoring repetition that communicates "I have the truth, you didn't get it yet, and you need to shape up" is unlikely to be winsome. I choose texts like Bakhtin's reflection on love and interpretation in part because they are evocative and challenging, in part because they point to ways in which we need to change, and in part because they articulate things that I am still learning myself. If the text is calling me to serious reflection and intentional response, that positions me alongside students on the road, inviting them into the rhythms of a shared journey. We can talk about how we are trying to respond, instead of me talking about how you should respond.

Repetition may help retention and reinforce mastery of key course concepts. Yet the kinds of repetition I have been describing in these last three chapters are not quite the same as the kind most often mentioned in literature on learning. The point here is not drilling. Front and center among my concerns are what students glean from course rhythms and what intentional practices they are offered in which they can repeatedly work on their formation. If I want my students to grow into a nuanced sense of how faith can inform learning and life, a recurring dialogue and an iterative, shared attempt to live out challenging truths in our immediate learning practices offer a more promising road to travel than the occasional admonition or devotional flourish.

Exercises

- Read this chapter again slowly, looking for details, connections, or possible applications that you may have missed the first time through. Pause at intervals to reflect on why these ideas were chosen and to focus on possible implications for your own teaching. What did you notice about how this chapter connects Christian faith and teaching that was less clear to you the first time you read it?
- Divide a page in two. On the left, list the skills and ideas your students work on again and again in the assignments in your class. On the right list your deep hopes for student growth and flourishing during your class. How are the two lists related? Should they be more closely aligned in any way?
- Return to the second exercise of the last chapter and the hope for students that you articulated there. Look for a significant quotation or paragraph from something you have read that articulates that hope succinctly and winsomely. A text that has inspired or shaped your own thinking is a good place to look. Choose a quotation that challenges you and could have implications for the class's learning practices if it were taken seriously. Outline a plan for weaving it repeatedly into your course without the repetition becoming mechanical or overbearing. Share your notes with a colleague and a student for feedback.

ENDING

THINKING BACKWARD

I began the first main chapter of this book with the observation that every teacher has to begin. Ending is equally unavoidable. Every class period, unit sequence, course, semester, or year must be brought to a close. How we do so becomes part of the story our teaching tells.

Think of any iconic narrative and imagine it ending differently. Romeo settles down with Juliet and raises a family. Luke Skywalker fails to destroy the Death Star, and the rebellion is crushed. The seven samurai decide to join the bandits in exploiting the villagers. The *Titanic* limps into New York with all passengers and crew still aboard. Suppose the rest of the story is basically unaltered. Would you be hearing the same story? How might these endings make you understand earlier events differently? Tragedies might become comedies, or vice versa. Early signs of hope might become vain illusions. Omens of doom might be shown up as needless anxiety. Characters apparently destined to be heroes might turn out to be insignificant after all. The hunch that good triumphs over evil might turn out to have been wishful thinking. Endings confirm or transform our sense of what kind of story we have been following and what it all meant.

I have sometimes used a very short story by Bertolt Brecht in German classes.[1] Instead of asking students to read the story, I reveal it a sentence or two at a time, pausing for discussion after each installment.

The first sentences tell us the moral of the story, though students commonly forget this as soon as they get caught up in the events that follow. The opening lines announce that the story will be about the bad habit of letting an injustice that we have suffered eat at us in silence. The narrative then places us on a city street where a passing pedestrian asks a crying child why he is upset.

Before continuing, I ask students to discuss in pairs what they think will happen next. I gather several suggestions before moving on.

The crying boy explains that he had two coins and was going to buy a ticket to the cinema. Another boy, standing nearby, stole one of them from him. The man asks whether he called for help; the boy says that he did.

By this point, students are already somewhat invested, quite pleased if their initial prediction was close to what actually ensued. I ask them once more to predict what will happen next, and gather suggestions. We continue with the story.

The man asks the boy if anyone heard him, accompanying the question with a fond touch. The answer, through more tears, is no. The man asks if the boy could have shouted louder. Again, no. The boy is beginning to look hopeful.

We pause again. What happens next? My students often become less confident at this point. Is the man compassionate or creepy? Is this going to take a happy or an ugly turn? They offer various conjectures, though they rarely name the actual end of the story. I reveal the final sentence:

> "Then give me that one as well," said the man and took the second dime out of the boy's hand and walked away unconcerned.[2]

Many of my students are a little shocked; I often hear gasps. Some are outraged. Somehow even their own earlier suspicions that the man's fond caress might be predatory did not quite prepare them for the casual injustice of the finale. It turns out their cynicism was halfhearted; they wanted the story to affirm a moral order.

By this stage, the final twist is not just an academic exercise for them. Through repeated engagement in making predictions, putting themselves into the place of the storyteller and imagining the story moving forward, students have become personally invested in how the story goes, how it is supposed to end. Their sense of proper narrative shape has (as Brecht surely intended) been offended. That upset has (as Brecht also surely intended) forced to the surface their basic sense of justice. Even if bad things happen, the unjust are not supposed to blithely win in the end.

This leads us into a wider discussion. Why might Brecht have written the story this way? What was he telling us when he announced the story's theme at the beginning, and why did we give little thought to that announcement as we got invested in the story itself? What might Brecht be trying to provoke in us? Is he addressing our reluctance to speak up when injustice happens, or our frequent powerlessness in the face of injustice whether we speak up or not?

Ending as Teaching

My reason for describing this story here is to illustrate how an unexpected ending can disorient us, forcing us to momentarily reconsider our grasp of the world.[3] Endings may come last, but they cast a retrospective shadow over everything that came before. Change the ending, and we may even have an unsettling sense that our instinctive hopes for our lives, the script in which we live happily ever after, might be in some kind of jeopardy. Botch the ending, and what seemed like a promising story arc leaves us distressed. Until we see the ending, it remains unclear what kind of story we are in and whether it is worth telling.

When we react to an ending, we reveal something about our social imaginary, the underlying way we imagine how the world is supposed to go.[4] Many years ago, I tried another gradual narrative with a group of twelve-year-olds while teaching a Sunday school class. I used the story of the martyrdom of Polycarp, the earliest account of Christian martyrdom outside the pages of the New Testament. As with the Brecht class, I told the story in stages, pausing to invite the students to predict what would happen next. We progressed through Polycarp's arrest, his confrontation with the Roman governor, his conveyance into the arena, his attachment to a stake, and the heaping of firewood. I mentioned at the outset that it was a martyrdom story, yet to the very end the students kept predicting miraculous ways in which God would rescue Polycarp from the situation. None of them suggested he might die. Some features of the story may have encouraged this (the flames do not at first harm him, and a spear has to complete the job), but I also wondered how many movies they had watched in which the hero implausibly yet inevitably cheats death to get us to an ending in which all is set right. I wondered how much of the piety amid which they had been raised reflected a story in which God would make sure nothing bad happened to us, however much such things might happen to others. When we discover what ending we need the story to have to keep our sense of propriety intact, we discover something important about our worldview.

To be clear, I am not suggesting here that we assault students with an unjust ending to our courses in order to jolt them into reflection. I am simply pointing to endings as a final practice to ponder. Class sessions, units, courses, semesters, and school years all have endings. All too often they stumble to a close, with deadlines, exams, and grades serving as the main plot-resolving devices. What do our endings communicate about the kind of story we think we are inhabiting as we teach and learn?

Two schools in which I taught early in my teaching career gave me a glimpse of some radically divergent endings. In one, it seemed common practice for teachers to join students in basically giving up before the end of the school year. Showing a popular movie in class was a favored alternative to further learning, and the promised viewing was held out as the carrot to motivate the last few learning tasks. It felt less like a celebration of what had been achieved and more like a capitulation to the feeling that nobody would want to keep learning any longer than they had to. If there was still class time left, students would be left to do nothing as long as they were willing to sit tight until their time was served. In the other school, there was an intentional effort not to let the students' final year end with grades. The graduating sixteen-year-olds were invited to a banquet, for which they dressed up in formal evening wear. The explicit intention was to signal and celebrate that they were becoming adults. Each student was given cards on which they were asked to write messages to other students or teachers about what they had learned from them and what they appreciated about them. These were then delivered personally over the course of the evening. Teachers joined in and helped add messages to any student who might be neglected. The evening became a celebration of the role of the whole community in helping each student toward maturity.

When endings recur, students learn to look for them. Students' expectations about how we will finish tell us something about the story they have internalized about what their learning is for and where we are headed. I once heard a middle school teacher describe how she ended each day by formally speaking words of blessing and encouragement to her students. On one occasion, when she was caught up in the close of an intense activity and dismissed the class without the usual ending, a student came to her in apparent distress. "You didn't bless us today!" was the student's lament. The patterns in our habitual endings inform students' sense of what to expect. I wonder if teachers of the lowest age ranges might have the most to teach the rest of us about ways to bring learning to an end that are rooted in a holistic vision of students' thriving.

Until relatively recently I gave much more thought to how my classes and courses began than to how they ended. I knew that the first day of class mattered, that setting expectations and trajectories was important, but endings were more like a race to wrap up the loose ends and stagger across the finish line, not an occasion to think about what story I was telling. That was shortsighted. The way we finish casts a shadow back across the semester. It tells students what we think we have been doing.

One way or another, it matters what happens in the end.

Exercises

- Reflect on courses you experienced as a student. How did they typically end? What did that ending communicate to you about the nature of learning and how you should think about your education? Were there any unusual endings that sparked different perceptions?
- Summarize to a colleague in your own words why thinking about endings might be a relevant exercise if we want to think about how Christian faith can inform teaching.
- Think ahead to the next semester. Write some notes on the key messages you would like students to take away from their learning. Then identify a way of beginning the course and a way of ending it that might convey those messages. Focus on how the beginning and the ending cohere. Then consider how both might cohere with your response to the last exercise on page 168.

SEEKING CONGRUENCE

Many years ago, I was part of the Charis curriculum project, a project that set out to design learning materials that targeted moral and spiritual development across the curriculum.[1] Keith Heywood, a fellow teacher educator and Charis team member, developed a teaching unit for the high school German classroom based on the life of a family friend.[2] The unit is structured around the life story of Adaline Kelbert, an elderly German housewife living in Hamburg. For many years I continued to adapt it for my own classroom.[3] I want to focus on how the unit ends, but first I need to give you a sense of how we get to the ending, so bear with me while I tell a little of the story that gets us there.[4]

The Story before the Ending

Adaline was born into a German-speaking family near Kyiv in 1903. In 1916 the family had to leave their home because of the First World War. They traveled east, moving from one village to the next until they eventually found hospitality in a Tartar village near Omsk in Siberia. Their hosts had a two-room log house and gave up one room to the refugee family. There was no work for them, and so the family moved farther to a German-speaking Mennonite village. In 1918 they were able to return to their hometown and get their farm running again. Adaline married a young man from a neighboring village in 1923. In the ensuing years they faced increasing demands for grain from the new communist authorities, until finally, in 1930, the family were told that they must hand over their farm. One evening men came and took everything, leaving Adaline in an empty house. Her husband was imprisoned for five years for unapproved trading, and then the house too was demanded. Adaline and her four children moved into a two-room house with her sister-in-law. Her husband was sent to work in Dnepropetrovsk but ran away and returned home, living in hiding at an aunt's house for some time. In 1933–1934, failed crops drove the family to migrate once more, to Odessa and back, finally settling on a collective farm. During the Second World War the German army passed through, identified the family as German speakers, and sent them to Germany. The husband and two sons were conscripted into the German army, while Adaline lived for several weeks in a local school, writing letters to try to trace her family. Her husband and the surviving older son were reunited with her in the summer of 1945, and the family settled in Pinneberg, a town near Hamburg. At the end of a recorded interview in which she narrates her life story, Adaline reflects that when the family was fleeing, there was always "this trust, there is One there who cares for all our cares . . . and when things were still so dark, some spark was always there that gave one comfort and new courage again."[5]

The teaching resources built around this story include family photographs, a recorded interview with Adaline, and various activities and worksheets. When I taught the unit, I typically began with the photographs, using them to draw students into the story and as a stimulus for speaking practice. Lingering over each picture to build up a sense of time, place, feeling, and motive began to make Adaline real to students. The photographs alone added a dimension to my class that had been largely missing from my lower-level language courses. The language textbooks available to me were typically populated by images of young and affluent people shopping, vacationing, and engaging in expensive hobbies. In this unit, the images were of an elderly lady celebrating her fiftieth wedding anniversary, a rural funeral, a family journey by horse and cart, family snapshots of people of modest means. This life story included displacement, bereavement, suffering, and the hope and courage with which these were met. Its contours felt like a gain over the blithe consumerism of more mainstream resources.

As the story unfolded and we practiced understanding past-tense narrative, more opportunities for fresh reflection arose. When Adaline remembers the time in the Mennonite village near Omsk, she comments, "We lived well there." She mentions the availability of bread, milk, work, a roof over their head, and a church that spoke their language. I invited students to reflect in pairs on the five things they might list as the basis for describing a time when they "lived well"; we made lists, shared them, and compared them to Adaline's. When we saw Adaline's family taken in by a Tartar family living in a two-room log cabin, we reflected together on how many of us, with our vastly more spacious houses, were ready to take in a family in need from a different culture and language. When we looked at a room in Adaline's house at the end of her life, with an array of family photos on display, we wondered what might be most important to us if we lived to be ninety-three, and how that might affect our present choices. These are strikingly different questions from the ones most often modeled by my regular language textbooks ("How much is a train ticket to Hamburg?" "What is your favorite food?" "What did you do at the weekend?"). Working with Adaline's life story seems to naturally give rise to questions that have some potential for spiritual and moral engagement. Working with narratives about a weekend trip to the beach does not typically have the same effect.

Working with Adaline's story also offered chances to frame mundane learning tasks in fresh ways. Midway through the story, I assigned students to learn the past-tense forms of a set of irregular verbs. Because they are irregular, there are few shortcuts; they have to be memorized, which for most students is not the most exciting moment in the language-learning process. Why should they invest time in it? During my own schooling, I heard variants on "you just have to do this." Adaline's story allowed me to frame the task differently. "Tomorrow," I told students, "we will listen to her telling the next part of her story. She will use a number of these verbs. If we don't learn them, we risk misunderstanding what she has to tell us. That would be a failure of care on our part." This feels like a more meaningful rationale than "it's painful but it was done to me and you have to submit to it too." Grammar can serve respect, and learning a new language is as much about learning to listen well to voices that were previously marginal to us as it is about our own voices.

In these various concrete ways, the story let me avoid a kind of idealistic dishonesty about my goals. I taught for years in school language programs where our vision statements talked in idealistic terms about language learning breaking down barriers between cultures while our curriculum mostly practiced talking about ourselves and engaging in consumer activities. More recently I have sought ways to make my students aware that I view language learning as related to the biblical call to exercise hospitality to strangers and to love our neighbor as ourselves—I talked about this in an earlier chapter (pp. 73–78). We learn the languages of others not just to bolster our career chances, meet academic requirements, or have better vacations, but because the humans who speak those languages should matter to us. This sets me up for potential inconsistency. If I articulate this rationale and we then spend most of our class time rehearsing talk about ourselves and consumer behavior, my words and my deeds diverge, and the framing talk will begin to sound hollow. If I am going to use Christian talk, I want it to be genuine commentary on what we are doing, not a superficial gloss to remind ourselves that we are pious. Spending significant class time learning to listen to an obscure, elderly, German lady telling her life story seems like the kind of move that might give me permission to keep talking about hospitality to strangers as the ground for what we are doing.

Fitting Endings

I trust that you have been waiting patiently for me to get back to the matter of how all of this ends. How does everything I just described help us to think about endings, and how they might connect to faith?

By the end of this unit, we had spent almost two weeks of classes talking about photographs and maps, reading sections of the narrative, listening to the recordings, and practicing past-tense narrative in speaking and writing tasks. All of this created a narrative trajectory that pressed me toward the question of how to bring it all to a fitting conclusion. Of course, Adaline's narrative had an ending, and we ran out of recordings and texts. But what about the pedagogical story?

What if the last act in this sequence were a traditional grammar test in which students comprehend and produce a series of sentences in the past tense, perhaps sentences pulled from the story? That would meet some of the learning goals and seem pretty normal to students. But how might that ending lead us to read backward across the work that went before it? If what will be on the test is how students infer what matters, what would they glean from such an ending? Might it suggest that Adaline's story was really just a pretext for schoolwork, a convenient illustration to help sweeten the pill of formal learning tasks? Might it imply that even though we were pursuing multiple goals and interests, the one that really counted was grammatical mastery, while the others were a kind of hopeful haze accompanying the main show? Might it reinforce the suspicion that the life we studied was in the end mostly a means to a grade?

What if I ended by asking students to write a reflection on how language learning could be a way to love our neighbor and practice hospitality to the stranger, perhaps with biblical references? That might get at some of my framing concerns, and it might fit the practices of some specific kinds of school, but might it imply that as long as we add the right Christian commentary at the end, remembering vocabulary and mastering grammar do not really matter so much? Might it suggest that as long as we end with the right sentiments, the competence we were aiming for is not so vital?

In the actual final assignment, I asked students to identify an elderly person to interview in English. This could be a family member, but if anyone was stuck there was a retirement village very close to our campus. We used a set of interview questions structured around the themes of Adaline's story. We asked about major life experiences, what made certain times difficult, and where hope was found. In class, after the interviews, students summarized their findings orally in German in small groups. Then they wrote an account in German of their interviewee's life. This let me assess their mastery of the past tense. It also created opportunities for cultural comparisons, allowed local elderly people to retell cherished stories to a fresh audience, and gave my students a chance to practice listening well to the elderly. Some students discovered episodes in the lives of their own relatives of which they had been ignorant. One year, a student learned for the first time through this task that her grandfather had patented an invention. Might this ending keep alive the story thread that says yes, we are learning words, grammar, and communication skills, and we are also learning to love our neighbor, to honor others, to be hospitable, to listen well to people who are not us?

I cannot know for sure how this has played out in the mind and memory of each of my students. What I am describing is not surefire technique or the one right way to end, but an attempt to craft an ending that sustains and remains true to the pedagogical story I was trying to tell. It is just one example of a recurring quest for endings that might be plausible extensions of what I believe about who we are called to be.

Exercises

- Look back over the specific pedagogical moves detailed in this chapter: the choice of unit topic, the choice of images, the choice of questions, the rationale for grammar learning, and the choice of ending. For each one, describe explicitly how it seems to have been influenced by Christian concerns. Consider whether the connections to faith that are named or implied are plausible. Think of at least one different direction that could have been taken based on the same starting convictions.
- The next time you conclude your teaching of a topic, ask students in the next class session to describe back to you how the previous sequence ended and what lessons they drew from that ending about what you valued most in their learning.
- Choose a substantive topic that you teach, one that takes more than a week. Draw two columns. On the left, name your goals and your hopes for the sequence—what do you most want to communicate and how do you want students to engage and grow? On the right, identify your current strategies for bringing the sequence to a close and for assessing the learning that has taken place. Where do you notice a sense of fit between the two columns? Where do you notice tensions? Is there anything you should consider changing?

JUDGING AND BLESSING

The moment that really got me thinking more intensively about endings came several years ago, during a conversation with a colleague. We were talking about liturgy and its points of contact with pedagogy.[1] As we chased ideas this way and that, it struck me that there is quite a contrast in how church liturgies and the ritual rhythms of college classes typically end.

In church, a worship service commonly ends with a blessing and a commission. The last two utterances are usually variants of "the Lord bless you and keep you" and "go in peace to love and serve the Lord." God's favor is spoken over us, and we are nudged into anticipation that we will continue to walk and grow in faith amid the tasks and opportunities ahead. The immediate liturgy is over, but its trajectory is not finished. Next comes service grounded in grace.

University classes in my experience typically end with a judgment and a dismissal. Even if food or stories are shared during the final week of class, this is usually followed by a silent exam and a grade posted online. After those two moves, students are released from further obligation. Quentin Schultze describes the experience of witnessing one student ceremonially dump his binder of notes in the trash at the end of the exam, dramatically enacting the sense that the exam is not just an ending but a severing of relevance.[2] At this point, the notes can be recycled, the textbooks can be returned, the grade has been banked, the instructor has lost their power, and the episode is over.

A science or history class is not a worship service, nor should it become one. Yet like a church service, a class has a ritual shape that speaks to us of who we are, how our world is put together, and how we are to insert ourselves into the world's story. The message is not just in the words.

In a course, as in a church service, the ending tells us what kind of story we are in.

The starkness of the church/school contrast got me thinking, and I began to change how several of my classes ended. I have tried out variants in different classes. I'll focus here on a class on language pedagogy for future teachers of world languages. As always, the point is not for you to shoehorn my strategy into your different classes and circumstances. The point is to think about what we are saying with our endings and how faith frames what we say.

One of my first thoughts when designing the class was that the ability to write essays or answer questions is a poor indicator of students' competence as language teachers. As a final assessment, therefore, I have students work collaboratively on designing teaching sequences for their future language classrooms. At the end of the semester they present these to an audience of peers and invited local educators. Thinking about liturgical endings led me to make some changes (with administrative permission) to how this particular ending unfolds.

What I do now goes like this. I schedule the final student presentations for the last class session before exam week. I let students know that this is not the final meeting; we still have a slot on the exam schedule for the following week, and we will still use it or an alternative time, with attendance expected. In fact, we usually end up meeting at different times. It is usually possible to negotiate a final meeting time that works better for everyone earlier in the week. I have also learned through trial and error that this final session works much better if I divide the class into groups of six or so and meet each group separately rather than meeting with the whole class at once. This commits me to some extra time but also makes flexible scheduling much easier. I suspect it also makes it feel more important to the students that they show up, as an absence will be less anonymous.

The first time I tried this sequence, only two-thirds of the students showed up. The rest had apparently correctly identified the thorough lack of consequences for not attending. Whether because of the smaller groups, a better job on my part of explaining why it matters, or an unusual run of exceptionally virtuous students, for a number of years now I have had close to perfect attendance at the last meetings. Your mileage may vary, and the demands of scheduling in your context may point toward an entirely different solution.

Closing Questions

At the final meeting I use five questions to structure a conversation, inviting each student in turn to respond to them. There is explicit freedom to pass if they so choose.

1. What was the most significant learning moment or process for you during the semester? Why was it significant? Why did it work?
2. What is one thing you learned this semester that you do not want to lose hold of going forward? How can you carry it forward? What are your strategies for not letting it slip away?
3. What is one thing from this semester that you glimpsed but are still working on, something you still need to learn? How might you continue working on it?
4. What is one thing I did that did not help your learning? What is one way in which the course could be improved pedagogically to help next year's students?
5. What challenges do you face in the coming weeks and months? What makes you anxious about next semester? How can I pray for you?

Several intentions lie behind these questions.

For one thing, I am educating future teachers and the course is about pedagogy. This exercise gives us one last chance to think explicitly together about the forms of teaching and learning in which we have been immersed. This is not the first time we have done this. Throughout the semester I have regularly paused and asked students to unpick what we just did together and examine whether it seemed like a good way to teach. With this foundation in place, they can now continue to extend their skill at identifying what was fruitful and why. As teachers, ongoing learning and self-awareness will be vital to their flourishing and to that of their students. My sense is that a fitting ending for this course should focus on continuing growth and reflection more than task completion and banking of credit. Questions 1 and 4 in particular are targeted toward this.

My students' need for ongoing learning is mirrored in my own, and this conversation also allows me to model an ending that shows continuing reflection on my teaching. No matter how many times I teach the course, I still find ways it can be improved, sometimes significantly. Students always have thoughtful and constructive suggestions. On one recent occasion, this exchange led me to abandon the textbook we had been using and seek alternatives. We do have written course evaluations, but they rarely give me the kind of insight into students' experience of the course that can come from our final conversation. Questions 1–4 all help me to learn about my teaching; question 4 lets students see that happening.

I have liturgical questions in mind too. The impulse that set all of this in motion came from reflecting on the difference between ending with a blessing/commission and ending with a judgment/dismissal. That train of thought is most explicit in question 5, with its explicit blessing and commission, but I hope that this does not come as an awkward appendage to the rest of the sequence. In the preceding questions, I have intentionally sought to model humility and an active care for my students' continuing growth. I have intentionally communicated that the semester's learning is not over but needs to be carried forward if we are to serve well in our callings. When we get to question 5, I hope that pausing to receive care and gather hope for what comes next fits the inner logic of where we have been headed. After students have shared their fears, concerns, and immediate future plans, I ask permission to pray for them, then I thank them for their work and send them off into the break with simple words of blessing. My sense from students' comments is that most experience this last chance to be heard and encouraged as a concluding blessing more than a final chore.

Of course, your class may need to end quite differently. We are still not aiming to find the perfect strategy, but to get practice in spotting links between faith and teaching. In this instance, a conversation about liturgies started a train of thought that ended up reshaping how my semesters end. The words of the church's liturgy did not tell me exactly how to end a language pedagogy course, nor did they give me evidence that my experiment is the right answer. They did offer me a glimpse of the proper shape of things and a sense of direction. The rest involves finding ways of relating that sense of the wholeness of things to a specific context and then being attentive to what unfolds.

I remain intrigued by Abraham Heschel's notion of an "architecture of time," a way of shaping our movement through time together to reflect and nurture our faith rather than just crunching in mechanical increments from one task to the next.[3] It's relatively easy to think of faith as affecting our words, our character, our relationships; does it affect how we shape time? How would students experience learning differently if classes typically ended with reflection together on how we have changed, how we still need to change, and how we might bless one another going forward? This is one last iteration of the questions about faith and teaching that we have been pursuing throughout this book. We shape time by beginning, connecting, framing, assigning, pausing, repeating, and ending. We can approach these moves as mechanical increments conveying us from one week and from one semester to the next. We can also approach them as architecture, as the creation of a pedagogical home whose shape and texture, though different in each time and place, are plausible extensions of what we hold to be true and who we are called to be. If Christian faith can help shape an architecture of time, then it can help us reflect on how to end well.

Exercises

- Think of a typical church service and list moments where humility, connection to one another, confession, joy, gratitude, receptiveness, hope, compassion, or commissioning are enacted. Then consider a course you teach through the lens of your list. Do not attempt to mechanically apply the items; your class is not and should not be a church service. Rather, look for any resonances or contrasts that might nudge you to see your course in a fresh way.
- Focus on one class you are currently teaching. Make a plan for ending it in a way that might be experienced as a blessing and commission.
- How should this book end?

CLOSE

ORBIS PICTUS: CLOSE

LEARN TO BE WISE

"Come, child! Learn to be wise."

We began this book where Comenius began his *Orbis Pictus*, standing alongside a student by a road that led to a town, pointing to the light and ready to walk together along a path of discipline, learning, and service (see the image on the facing page). I described in an earlier chapter (pp. 85–91) how the *Orbis Pictus* proceeds through an array of creatures, callings, virtues, faiths, and trials and ends with a chapter on the final judgment. That might seem to bode ill for this last chapter. But after the whole sequence of topics, after the chapter on judgment, comes one more section, brief and unnumbered, addressed directly to the reader. It is titled simply "The Close." Like the other chapters, it is built around an image.

The picture is, of course, the same one that greeted us on the opening page. Given Comenius's lavish investment in over 150 detailed woodcut images for the rest of the book, I don't think the repetition is motivated by economizing. We are supposed to notice that at the end, we are still in some important ways where we started. The text beneath reads: "Thus thou hast seen in short all things that can be shewed, and hast learned the chief Words of the English and Latine Tongue. Go on now and read other good Books diligently, and thou shalt become learned, wise, and godly. Remember these things: fear God, and call upon him, that he may bestow upon thee the Spirit of Wisdom. Farewell."[1]

After everything that has preceded, we find ourselves standing by the same road, hearing the same invitation: seek further, grow more, learn to be wise. Modern printing gave us a period of history in which we learned to imagine that understanding could be contained between two covers and held in our hands; the message here points in a different direction.[2] The book was just a helper along a road that we must continue to travel together outside its pages. What seemed at times like an encyclopedia ("all things that can be shewed") turns out to be a primer ("read other good Books") and an admonition ("fear God, and call upon him"). Godliness is not something conquered and bottled in a course of study, nor is there hope without calling on God and receiving the Spirit of Wisdom. Mastering the book was an important learning step, but in the end not the point.

So with this book, though it cannot measure up to the *Orbis Pictus* and has not made the slightest attempt to show all things that can be showed. I have set out neither to survey every way in which teaching can be Christian nor to provide examples for every classroom, age group, and discipline. I have offered neither a method with steps to be followed nor a set of proven best practices to be copied wholesale. Rather, I have tried in my own limited fashion to offer concrete ways of getting used to thinking about faith and teaching, ways that do not boil down to praying in class or trying to be a nice person, worthwhile as both of those impulses may be. I have not set out to identify teaching strategies that are uniquely Christian or that only Christians could use, but rather to show how starting from Christian beliefs and instincts can shape the choices we make and the pedagogical homes we construct. Like the teacher in the picture, I stand at a particular spot by the road, and I have drawn most from the kinds of teaching I know best and the examples I have reflected on longest. The landscape by your stretch of the road likely looks a little different. You have your own journey toward wisdom, and I have only offered to walk a little way in conversation with you, not to walk it for you.

I hope that some of what you have reflected on while reading leads to constructive change, but I am not inviting you to change everything at once. At this point I suggest getting a drink and a snack and perhaps going back to one part of the book that intrigued you in some way. Give some time to reflecting again on connections you could make between the ideas there and your own classroom, accepting that they may differ from the connections I made. Make a plan. Discuss it with a friend. Try it out. Reflect on what happened. Ask students how it went. Read another book that connects faith and teaching (there are some examples below) and think about how its strategies are similar to or different from those you have found here. Then begin again and try out another connection.

In the end, making connections is how you become fluent at making connections.

The road still stretches ahead of us. As we continue to walk it, may God bestow upon you the Spirit of wisdom as you fashion fruitful learning for your students. May God strengthen what has been worked in you. May God's beauty be upon your students, and may the delightfulness of God attend you, and may he align the works of your hands.

Go on now, read other good books diligently, and learn to be wise.

GO ON NOW

Lest my parting exhortation land without sufficient practical support, I offer here a few brief suggestions of places to turn next.

The following is neither a complete list of books on Christian faith and teaching nor an endorsed list of those with the correct answers. They are chosen because they reflect varied age levels, Christian theological identities, and approaches to connecting faith and teaching. They might therefore offer further material for exploring and questioning the nature of that connection and identifying the strengths and weaknesses of different approaches.

- Cooling, Trevor, et al. *Christian Faith in English Church Schools: Research Conversations with Classroom Teachers*. Bern: Lang, 2016.
- Eifler, Karen E., and Thomas M. Landy, eds. *Becoming Beholders: Cultivating Sacramental Imagination and Actions in College Classrooms*. Collegeville, MN: Liturgical Press, 2014.
- Glanzer, Perry, and Nathan Alleman. *The Outrageous Idea of Christian Teaching*. New York: Oxford University Press, 2019.
- Graham, Donovan. *Teaching Redemptively: Joining Jesus' Restoration Project in Your Classroom*. Colorado Springs: Purposeful Design Publications, 2023.
- Hughes, Kyle R. *Teaching for Spiritual Formation: A Patristic Approach to Christian Education in a Convulsed Age*. Eugene, OR: Cascade, 2022.
- Palmer, Parker J. *To Know as We Are Known: A Spirituality of Education*. San Francisco: Harper & Row, 1983.
- Swaner, Lynn E., and Andy Wolfe. *Flourishing Together: A Christian Vision for Students, Educators, and Schools*. Grand Rapids: Eerdmans, 2021.

At the Kuyers Institute for Christian Teaching and Learning at Calvin University, where I work, we have developed a number of online projects intended to offer practical examples of teachers making teaching choices in light of their Christian commitments. As with all the other examples discussed here, these examples are not presented as perfect models, but rather as a chance to see how others are making connections. You can explore several hundred examples across a range of ages and subject areas at the following addresses:

whatiflearning.com
teachfastly.com
civichospitality.com
pedagogy.net

If you would like to explore professional development possibilities around this topic, for yourself or for teachers you lead, you may find helpful a new collection of online training resources that are in development alongside this book at www.everydaychristianteaching.com.

ACKNOWLEDGMENTS

Even more than most books, books about teaching are the product of myriad interactions with others. I am very grateful to Eun Hee Yoo, Julia Smith, Lydia Chu, and Robert Keeley for reading part or all of the manuscript and providing valuable feedback and moral support. Emily Reisler contributed some timely input on overall organization, and Michele Rau helped me catch various small errors. I am also grateful to Joyce Azaki Nash for her willingness to contribute her learning experiences to the chapter "Pausing for Hospitality" in PAUSING. As is apparent in specific ways in many of the chapters, the efforts of a range of colleagues to develop Christian approaches to their teaching work have fed into the story told here. Students in several of my classes at Calvin University have been subjected to some of the pedagogical experiments described here and have shared helpful reflections on them; the voices of some of them appear directly in several chapters, while many more are implicit in the background. The opportunity to develop and teach a new course at Calvin University titled "The Christian Teacher" has provided a helpful context for working through the ideas in some chapters and a rich vein of student reflection. I am indebted to the many schools and universities in several countries that have given me opportunities to try out the ideas in this book with audiences of teaching faculty over several years.

The summer 2023 writing cooperative sponsored by the Calvin Center for Christian Scholarship was invaluable as a way of carving out time to complete a first full draft of the manuscript. My thanks go to David Urban and James Skillen for leading the retreat, as well as to the other participants for daily fellowship to punctuate our extended time of communion with our keyboards.

Some material in a number of the chapters has been reworked from parts of articles published in *Christian Educators Journal*, *Christian Teachers Journal*, *International Journal of Christianity and Education*, *Journal of Christianity and World Languages*, and the *Christ Animating Learning Blog*. Parts of the chapters in CONNECTING appear in adapted and expanded form in a chapter prepared at the same time as this book for the volume *Habits of Hope: Educational Practices for a Weary World*, edited by Todd C. Ream, Jerry Pattengale, and Christopher J. Devers (InterVarsity Press). Some material in the chapter "Small Pauses" in PAUSING overlaps with a chapter prepared for the volume *"A Tree of Life to Those Who Embrace Her": Reflections on the Pursuit of Wisdom and the Promise of Education in Honour of Doug Blomberg*, edited by Agnes A. Struik and Nicholas Ansell (Wipf & Stock).

Unless otherwise indicated, quotations from the Bible are from Today's New International Version.

This book follows on from the earlier volume *On Christian Teaching*, the title of which I borrowed from Augustine. Between that book and now I collaborated on a book titled *Digital Life Together*, a nod to Bonhoeffer. In this book you will find places where I lean on Comenius, Bakhtin, or Bernard of Clairvaux. Aside from the obvious point that there are those in our past who have thought more profoundly about the difference Christ makes to the world than I have been able to, I also intend these connections as signals that teaching and learning are not just about practical tips for after we are done discussing the big ideas. Teaching and learning are themselves worthy of the best thinking and the most thoughtful faith we can apply, and such thinking takes place in the company of our forebears. None of us think well alone.

NOTES

INVITATION: Invitation to Wisdom

1. The book is the *Orbis Sensualium Pictus* (Visible World in Pictures), first published in 1658. Curiously, in the edition from which the image is taken here the parallel German title is "Introduction" (*Einleitung*) rather than "Invitation" (*Einladung*), perhaps a testament to the weight of custom. The copy that I have used for citations from the text is John Amos Comenius, *Joh. Amos Comenius's Visible World*, trans. Charles Hoole (London: John Sprint, 1705). The images I have used are the same as those in that edition but have been drawn from the high-quality reproductions available at Wikimedia Commons (https://commons.wikimedia.org) of the 1658 Nuremberg edition (John Amos Comenius, *Orbis Sensualium Pictus* [Nuremberg: Michael Endter, 1658]). For this first image, see https://commons.wikimedia.org/wiki/File:Orbis-pictus-002.jpg. For background on the various details in this opening picture in its seventeenth-century context and further interpretation, see Ayers Bagley, "An Invitation to Wisdom and Schooling," University of Minnesota, 2010, http://iconics.cehd.umn.edu/OrbisSensualiumPictus/Lecture/default.html; Gerhard Michel, "Die Bedeutung des Orbis Sensualium Pictus für Schulbücher im Kontext der Geschichte der Schule," *Pedagogica Historica* 28, no. 2 (1992): 235–51; James Turner, "The Visual Realism of Comenius," *History of Education* 1, no. 2 (1972): 113–38; Jeong-Gil Woo, "Revisiting Orbis Sensualium Pictus: An Iconographical Reading in Light of the Pampaedia of J. A. Comenius," *Studies in Philosophy and Education* 35, no. 2 (2016): 215–33. The summary here draws from my previous overview in David I. Smith, *John Amos Comenius: A Visionary Reformer of Schools* (Camp Hill, PA: Classical Academic Press, 2017).

2. The imagery here matches one of Comenius's articulations (in his *Di-*

dactica Magna) of the central goals of education. He wrote that "humans have a genuine need to I. have knowledge of all things, II. have power over things and themselves, III. return themselves and all things to God, the source of everything. If we express these three with three generally familiar words, they are: I. Learning; II. Virtue, or worthy morals; III. Religion, or piety" (*Didactica Magna* 4.6, my translation). John Amos Comenius, *Opera Didactica Omnia*, vol. 1 (Prague: Academia Scientiarum Bohemoslovenica, 1957), 20.

INVITATION: Walking the Road

1. In one study of teachers in Christian schools in the United Kingdom, the majority of the participants "agreed that the number of teachers in the school who were Christians had a significant impact on the Christian nature of the school BUT the same teachers thought that it would be unprofessional to act specifically as Christian teachers rather than just as teachers who happened to be Christian." The same study found that school leaders believed that they had provided resources to help teachers to explore the Christian nature of the school, but that teachers did not feel that they had received such help and did not see the topic as part of their mentoring of new teachers. Trevor Cooling et al., *Christian Faith in English Church Schools: Research Conversations with Classroom Teachers* (Bern: Lang, 2016), 108–9.

2. Unless otherwise indicated, all quotations from the Bible in this book come from Today's New International Version.

3. John Calvin, *Golden Booklet of the True Christian Life* (Grand Rapids: Baker Books, 1952), 21.

4. David I. Smith, *On Christian Teaching: Practicing Faith in the Classroom* (Grand Rapids: Eerdmans, 2018). In the present book, as in *On Christian Teaching*, for the sake of simplicity I am going to take the term "pedagogy" to stand in for andragogy (teaching adults), heutagogy (teaching self-determining learners), and any other more specific kind of -gogy we might want to distinguish. While the etymology of the word indicates teaching children, "pedagogy" can be and commonly has been taken as a broader term for actions intended to produce learning.

5. This three-part framework for thinking about faith-informed planning for learning is explained at length in David I. Smith, *On Christian Teach-*

ing, 68–127. It is also the framework that informs the collection of examples at https://whatiflearning.com/.

6. Parker J. Palmer, *To Know as We Are Known: A Spirituality of Education* (San Francisco: Harper & Row, 1983), 30.

7. Jane Roland Martin notes the tendency in the history of Western culture to elide the home or ask it to conform to the pattern of the school, rather than asking how homes are educational. Jane Roland Martin, "The Love Gap in the Educational Text," in *Teaching, Learning, and Loving: Reclaiming Passion in Educational Practice*, ed. Daniel Liston and Jim Garrison (New York: RoutledgeFalmer, 2004), 21–34.

INVITATION: Pilgrim Practices

1. Cf. Dorothy C. Bass et al., *Christian Practical Wisdom: What It Is, Why It Matters* (Grand Rapids: Eerdmans, 2016).

2. Mark D. Jordan, *Transforming Fire: Imagining Christian Teaching* (Grand Rapids: Eerdmans, 2021), vi. See also David I. Smith, "Writing about Teaching," *International Journal of Christianity & Education* 27, no. 2 (2023): 117–20; Bram de Muynck, Bram Kunz, and Piet Murre, "Learning from Predecessors: Disclosing the Inspiring Potential of Historical Educators," *International Journal of Christianity and Education* 26, no. 2 (2022): 107–11.

3. I am indebted to my colleagues Jim Jadrich and Crystal Bruxvoort for input on this topic.

4. See, e.g., John Dunlosky et al., "Improving Students' Learning with Effective Learning Techniques: Promising Directions from Cognitive and Educational Psychology," *Psychological Science in the Public Interest* 14, no. 1 (2013): 4–58; Henry L. Roediger III and Andrew C. Butler, "The Critical Role of Retrieval Practice in Long-Term Retention," *Trends in Cognitive Sciences* 15, no. 1 (2011): 20–27.

5. Dunlosky et al., "Improving Students' Learning with Effective Learning Techniques."

6. Cited in James Lang, *Small Teaching: Everyday Lessons from the Science of Learning* (Hoboken, NJ: Jossey-Bass, 2012), 84.

BEGINNING: The Courage to Begin

1. For more detail on Bernard's breaking-bread metaphor as applied to teaching, see David I. Smith, "Teaching Is Breaking Bread: Biblical Meta-

phor, Educational Vision, and Bernard's Evocation of Learning," *Journal of Christian Education* 55, no. 1 (2012): 29–36. On Bernard's use of imagery, see Luke Anderson, "The Rhetorical Epistemology in Saint Bernard's *Super Cantica*," in *Bernardus Magister: Papers Presented at the Nonacentenary Celebration of the Birth of Saint Bernard of Clairvaux*, ed. John R. Sommerfeldt (Spencer, MA: Cistercian Publications, 1992), 95–128; Duncan Robertson, "The Experience of Reading: Bernard of Clairvaux Sermons on the 'Song of Songs,' I," *Religion and Literature* 19, no. 1 (1987): 1–20.

2. Compare 1 Cor. 3:1–2.

3. Bernard of Clairvaux, *On the Song of Songs 1*, trans. Kilian J. Walsh (Spencer, MA: Cistercian Publications, 1971), 1.

4. Bernard, *On the Song of Songs 1*, 1.

5. Bernard, *On the Song of Songs 1*, 3.

6. Bernard, *On the Song of Songs 1*, 1.

7. Ted Cohen suggests that metaphors create a kind of intimacy through a process whereby the speaker offers an implicit invitation in the metaphor to view things a certain way, the hearer has to work at accepting it, and so a kind of attunement takes place. See Ted Cohen, "Metaphor and the Cultivation of Intimacy," in *On Metaphor*, ed. Sheldon Sacks (Chicago: University of Chicago Press, 1978), 1–10.

8. Bernard, *On the Song of Songs 1*, 3.

9. For more examples, see David I. Smith et al., *Teaching and Christian Imagination* (Grand Rapids: Eerdmans, 2016); Ken Badley and Harro Van Brummelen, *Metaphors We Teach By: How Metaphors Shape What We Do in Classrooms* (Eugene, OR: Wipf & Stock, 2012).

BEGINNING: Naming Names

1. Jacob Stratman, "What's in a Name: The Place of Recognition in a Hospitable Classroom," *International Journal of Christianity & Education* 19, no. 1 (2015): 27–37.

2. Zygmunt Bauman, *Life in Fragments: Essays in Postmodern Morality* (Oxford: Blackwell, 1995), 44–71.

3. Bauman, *Life in Fragments*, 50.

4. Bauman says that in most modern social contexts, our encounters with others "tend to be inconsequential in the sense of not leaving a lasting legacy of mutual rights and/or obligations in their wake" (*Life in Fragments*, 50).

5. Bauman, *Life in Fragments*, 50.

6. Bauman, *Life in Fragments*, 51.

7. Stratman, "What's in a Name," 30.

8. It is worth noting that Bauman specifies that we cannot "plan, plot, design, calculate the passage from being-with to being-for" (*Life in Fragments*, 52). Precisely because it depends on the personhood of another person, it is not something we can guarantee by technique. The person with whom we try to start a discussion may be more interested in their phone. Nevertheless, we can seek kinds of togetherness that are "hospitable and conducive" (50) to such encounters, and while there is no specific setting that can guarantee being-for (even a marriage bed can be merely transactional), "none wards off its happening either" (52); there is always potential for connection. Classrooms, among other settings, are places where being-for can creep out "from behind the back of being-with" (52), and we can make classrooms hospitable to the possibility.

9. Stratman, "What's in a Name," 30.

10. Stratman, "What's in a Name," 30.

11. Stratman, "What's in a Name," 31.

12. Stratman, "What's in a Name," 31.

13. Stratman ("What's in a Name," 33) recognizes and discusses the possibility that this could seem threatening to some students. His experience is that it rarely does. I suspect that tone and skill at connecting well with students are playing an important role.

14. See, e.g., Katelyn M. Cooper et al., "What's in a Name? The Importance of Students Perceiving That an Instructor Knows Their Names in a High-Enrollment Biology Classroom," *CBE Life Sciences Education* 16, no. 1 (2017): 1–13; Yvette Denise Murdoch, Lim Hyejung, and Alin Kang, "Learning Students' Given Names Benefits EMI Classes," *English in Education* 52, no. 3 (2018): 225–47.

15. Student reflection by Brooke Adelman, quoted with permission. Similar practices are described in more detail in A. Alexander Beaujean, "Observing a Master Teacher," in *Called to Teach: Excellence, Commitment, and Community in Christian Higher Education*, ed. Christopher Richman and J. Lenore Wright (Eugene, OR: Pickwick, 2020), 20–36.

BEGINNING: Goals, Covenants, and Hope

1. Quentin Schultze, *Servant Teaching: Practices for Renewing Christian Higher Education* (Grand Rapids: Edenridge, 2022), 74.

2. Schultze, *Servant Teaching*, 74.

3. Compare, e.g., Lindsay B. Wheeler, Michael Palmer, and Itiya Aneece, "Students' Perceptions of Course Syllabi: The Role of Syllabi in Motivating Students," *International Journal for the Scholarship of Teaching and Learning* 13, no. 3 (2019): n.p., https://doi.org/10.20429/ijsotl.2019.130307; Brett D. Jones and Xiao Zhu, "The Effects of a Syllabus on Students' Perceptions of the Motivational Climate in a Course," *International Journal for the Scholarship of Teaching and Learning* 16, no. 3 (2022): n.p., https://doi.org/10.20429/ijsotl.2022.160303.

4. On the difference between and relevance of hopes and expectations, see Nicholas Wolterstorff, "The Peculiar Hope of the Educator," in *Foundations of Education: A Christian Vision*, ed. Matthew Etherington (Eugene, OR: Wipf & Stock, 2014), 119–30.

5. See REPEATING, pp. 151–68. For discussion of learning tasks that foster charitable reading, see David I. Smith, "Reading Practices and Christian Pedagogy: Enacting Charity with Texts," in *Teaching and Christian Practices: Reshaping Faith and Learning*, ed. David I. Smith and James K. A. Smith (Grand Rapids: Eerdmans, 2011), 43–60; Rachel B. Griffis, Julie Ooms, and Rachel M. De Smith Roberts, *Deep Reading: Practices to Subvert the Vices of Our Distracted, Hostile, and Consumeristic Age* (Grand Rapids: Baker Academic, 2024).

6. See pp. 39–44.

BEGINNING: Starting the Story

1. The discussion of secularization in language textbooks in this chapter and later, on pp. 85–91, draws from David I. Smith, "Language Textbooks and Social Imaginaries: Secularization in the *Orbis Pictus* and *The London Vocabulary*," *Journal of Christianity and World Languages* 21 (2020): 73–95.

2. Comenius, *Orbis Sensualium Pictus*.

3. Kurt Pilz, *Johann Amos Comenius: Die Ausgaben des Orbis Sensualium Pictus; Eine Bibliographie* (Nuremberg: Stadtbibliothek, 1967).

4. H. G. Good, "The 'First' Illustrated School-Books," *Journal of Educational Research* 35, no. 5 (1942): 338–43.

5. *Didactica Magna* 4.6, my translation. Comenius, *Opera Didactica Omnia*.

6. First published in 1711, the copy from which I draw text and images here is the materially unchanged twenty-first edition from 1797. James Greenwood, *The London Vocabulary, English and Latin*, 21st ed. (London: A. Bettesworth, 1797). See also DeWitt Talmage Starnes, "The London Vocabulary and Its Antecedents," *Studies in English* 19 (1939): 114–38.

7. James Southall Wilson, "Best-Sellers in Jefferson's Day," *Virginia Quarterly Review* 36, no. 2 (1960): 222–37.

8. In later reworkings of the opening image in successive editions of the *Orbis Pictus* across the next two centuries, the teacher first becomes a seated figure in a study, albeit still dressed and apparently poised for travel, before finally becoming a firmly seated figure in an indoor robe and slippers.

9. Tracy D. Terrell, Erwin Tschirner, and Brigitte Nikolai, *Kontakte: A Communicative Approach*, 5th ed. (New York: McGraw Hill, 2004). This is not the most recent edition of *Kontakte*, but it is the one with which I am most familiar through classroom use.

10. Comenius, *Orbis Sensualium Pictus*, 2.

11. Cf. the discussion of "spiritual addition professors" in Perry Glanzer and Nathan Alleman, *The Outrageous Idea of Christian Teaching* (New York: Oxford University Press, 2019).

12. Charles Taylor, *A Secular Age* (Cambridge, MA: Belknap Press of Harvard University Press, 2007), 22.

13. Miroslav Volf, "Theology for a Way of Life," in *Practicing Theology: Beliefs and Practices in Christian Life*, ed. Miroslav Volf and Dorothy C. Bass (Grand Rapids: Eerdmans, 2002), 245–63, here 247, 260.

BEGINNING: Gathering for the Journey

1. David I. Smith, *On Christian Teaching*, 14–26.

2. We went on later in the semester to discuss the kind of material explored in CONNECTING below.

3. Jasmine Bos, EDUC 249 journal assignment, quoted with permission.

4. Hannah Walter, EDUC 249 journal assignment, quoted with permission.

5. Sage Winters, EDUC 249 journal assignment, quoted with permission.

6. Claire van Zelst, EDUC 249 journal assignment, quoted with permission.

7. Madelyn Joseph, EDUC 249 journal assignment, quoted with permission.

8. Aaron Jahn, EDUC 249 journal assignment, quoted with permission.

9. FengYang Sun, EDUC 249 journal assignment, quoted with permission.

10. Many of my students are preparing to teach in public schools, and one of my concerns as I prepared the course was not to imply that being a Christian teacher was only feasible in settings where public prayers could be offered and Bible verses quoted.

CONNECTING: Communion in Gifts and Graces

1. David Bridges, *Fiction Written under Oath? Essays in Philosophy and Educational Research* (Dordrecht: Kluwer, 2003), 1; David I. Smith, *On Christian Teaching*, 35.

2. See, e.g., Walter Leal Filho et al., "Impacts of COVID-19 and Social Isolation on Academic Staff and Students at Universities: A Cross-Sectional Study," *BMC Public Health* 21, article 1213 (2021), https://doi.org/10.1186/s12889-021-11040-z.

3. Westminster Confession 26, https://www.ligonier.org/learn/articles/westminster-confession-faith.

4. The Heidelberg Catechism asks, "is it enough then that we do not murder our neighbor . . . ?" and answers: "No." Rather, we are to "love our neighbors as ourselves, to be patient, peace-loving, gentle, merciful, and friendly toward them, to protect them from harm as much as we can." Heidelberg Catechism, Q & A 107, https://www.crcna.org/welcome/beliefs/confessions/heidelberg-catechism. For one more recent point of comparison, the Belhar Confession, emerging from Reformed churches in southern Africa, says that our reconciliation to one another is "both a gift and an obligation for the church of Jesus Christ; that through the working of God's Spirit it is a binding force, yet simultaneously a reality which must be earnestly pursued and sought." Belhar Confession 2, https://www.rca.org/about/theology/creeds-and-confessions/the-belhar-confession/.

5. Dietrich Bonhoeffer, *Life Together and Prayerbook of the Bible*, trans. James H. Burtness and Daniel W. Bloesch, Dietrich Bonhoeffer Works, vol. 5 (Minneapolis: Fortress, 1996), 34–36.

6. John Van Dyk notes that "too much teacher talk allows the spirit of individualism to flourish in a classroom. When students are listening to the teacher all the time, they have very little opportunity to interact with each other and to work on their task of helping to build a community in the classroom. Their concern will be limited to how they, as individuals, get the information straight and know how to regurgitate it to the teacher. There will be no responsibility for each other's learning." John Van Dyk, *Letters to Lisa: Conversations with a Christian Teacher* (Sioux Center, IA: Dordt Press, 1997), 61.

7. Elizabeth Lovelock, private communication, quoted with permission.

CONNECTING: The Performance of Duties

1. John M. G. Barclay, *Paul and the Power of Grace* (Grand Rapids: Eerdmans, 2020), 64.

2. Craig Dykstra, *Growing in the Life of Faith: Education and Christian Practices*, 2nd ed. (Louisville: Westminster John Knox, 2005), 45–46.

3. Marcia K. Everett, "'I Never Would Have Talked to This Person': The Power of an Assignment to Encourage Engagement," *Christian Higher Education* 22, no. 3–4 (2023): 212–30, https://www.tandfonline.com/doi/full/10.1080/15363759.2023.2219070.

4. It is possible to design such clusters so that there are some pieces required of everyone and key information is present in more than one reading, reducing the chances that important things will be missed because of one student's poor summary. Finding the overlaps and differences between the different sources provided can be part of the task. Students can also be given a short list of key points that they must cover.

5. Cf. David I. Smith et al., "Which Student Struggles Do We Help to Create?," *Christ Animating Learning Blog*, May 4, 2021, https://christianscholars.com/which-student-struggles-do-we-help-to-create/.

CONNECTING: Learning Community Practices

1. Material in this chapter also appears in David I. Smith, "'Arduous and Difficult to Obtain': Teaching as a Hopeful Educational Practice," in *Habits of Hope: Educational Practices for a Weary World*, ed. Todd C. Ream, Jerry

Pattengale, and Christopher J. Devers (Downers Grove, IL: InterVarsity Press, 2024).

2. For an overview of the project, see Rachael Baker, "Building a Thriving Research Team" (March 23, 2021), "Practicing Humility in the Sciences" (May 11, 2021), "The Vocation of Science" (June 3, 2021), and "Mentoring for the Cultivation of Virtue in the Sciences" (July 17, 2001), all posted at *Vocation Matters: Insights and Conversations from the Network for Vocation in Undergraduate Education (NetVUE)*, https://vocationmatters.org/author/rachaelabaker/.

3. Jeff Hemsley et al., "Collaboration Networks and Career Trajectories: What Do Metadata from Data Repositories Tell Us?" *Proceedings of the Association for Information Science and Technology* 59, no. 1 (2022): 100–110.

4. Barry Bozeman and Craig Boardman, *Research Collaboration and Team Science: A State-of-the-Art Review and Agenda* (Cham, Switzerland: Springer: 2014), cited in Hemsley et al., "Collaboration Networks," 110.

5. See, e.g., Daniel Stokols et al., "The Science of Team Science: Overview of the Field and Introduction to the Supplement," *American Journal of Preventive Medicine* 35, no. 2 Supplement (2008): S77–S89.

6. Amy Wilstermann, "Building Thriving Science Laboratory and Classroom Communities," *Christian Educators Journal* 62, no. 1 (October 2022): 10–13, here 12.

7. Rachael Baker, "Cultivating Space for Christian Practices in Our Science Classrooms," *Christian Educators Journal* 62, no. 1 (October 2022): 16–20, here 17.

8. Rachael Baker, "What Faith Has to Offer Science," *Christian Educators Journal* 62, no. 1 (October 2022): 3–4, here 4.

9. Julie E. Yonker, "Could Humility Be the Heart of Our Classroom Communities?" *Christian Educators Journal* 62, no. 1 (October 2022): 21–24, here 22.

10. Yonker, "Could Humility Be the Heart?," 22.

11. Abridged from Yonker, "Could Humility Be the Heart?," 23.

12. Personal communication; this data is not published at time of writing. See also Julie E. Yonker et al., "Relational Based Christian Practices of Gratitude and Prayer Can Positively Impact Christian College Students' Reported Prosocial Tendencies," *International Journal of Christianity and Education* 23, no. 2 (2019): 150–70.

13. Yonker, "Could Humility Be the Heart?," 24.

14. Baker, "What Faith Has to Offer," 3.
15. Yonker, "Could Humility Be the Heart?," 24.

CONNECTING: Community beyond the Classroom

1. Material in this chapter is adapted from David I. Smith, "Resisting Homework as Solitary Confinement," *Christian Teachers Journal* 22, no. 4 (December 2014): 14–17.

2. I wonder how many schools are connected to churches that include retirees who might find it rewarding to be part of such encounters.

3. I describe a task like this for older students on p. 180, and more examples can be found, for instance, in the FAST project resources. See https://teachfastly.com/activity-map/homework/ and https://teachfastly.com/activity-map/engaging-parents-and-the-wider-community/.

4. Cf. Cornelius Plantinga, *Not the Way It's Supposed to Be: A Breviary of Sin* (Grand Rapids: Eerdmans, 1995).

FRAMING: Speaking, Hearing, Hospitality

1. This chapter includes material reworked from David I. Smith, "Hearing, Speaking, Learning," *Christian Teachers Journal* 30, no. 1 (February 2022): 11–13.

2. *Luther Bibel 1912* (Conroe, TX: Digital Bible Society, 2016).

3. Walter Brueggemann, *A Commentary on Jeremiah: Exile and Homecoming* (Grand Rapids: Eerdmans, 1998).

4. Brueggemann, *A Commentary on Jeremiah*, 82.

5. Brueggemann, *A Commentary on Jeremiah*, 82.

6. Jer. 7:6–13.

7. While this story is unique, other students have also written to me to tell of occasions when their language skills created an opportunity to help someone access a service or calm a dispute. It seems reasonable to suspect that the way we talked about language learning in class influenced the kind of experiences that students felt worth reporting.

8. See David I. Smith et al., *Teaching and Christian Imagination* (Grand Rapids: Eerdmans, 2016).

9. The Civic Hospitality Project was developed by the Kuyers Institute for Christian Teaching and Learning and the Henry Institute for the Study of

Christianity and Politics at Calvin University. It can be explored at https://civichospitality.com/.

10. Kevin R. Den Dulk, "Civic Hospitality and the Challenges of/to Pluralism," *Christian Educators Journal* 63, no. 1 (2023): 13–18; Matthew Kaemingk, "Our Civics and God's Hospitality," *Christian Educators Journal* 63, no. 1 (2023): 9–12; Micah Watson, "Hospitality, Politics, and Human Nature," *Christian Educators Journal* 63, no. 1 (2023): 22–25.

11. See, e.g., Christine D. Pohl, *Making Room: Recovering Hospitality as a Christian Tradition* (Grand Rapids: Eerdmans, 1999); Joshua W. Jipp, *Saved by Faith and Hospitality* (Grand Rapids: Eerdmans, 2017); Luke Bretherton, *Hospitality as Holiness: Christian Witness amid Moral Diversity* (Aldershot, UK: Ashgate, 2006); Luke Bretherton, *A Primer in Christian Ethics: Christ and the Struggle to Live Well* (Cambridge: Cambridge University Press, 2023).

12. Den Dulk, "Civic Hospitality and the Challenges of/to Pluralism."

13. Kelli Boender, "Don't Be a Jonah," *Christian Educators Journal* 63, no. 1 (2023): 35–38.

14. This lesson is described in detail at https://civichospitality.com/topic/stories/.

15. Boender, "Don't Be a Jonah," 37.

16. Boender, "Don't Be a Jonah," 38.

FRAMING: Coding and Beauty

1. For a helpful orientation to this question, see David Klanderman et al., "Faith Integration in STEM Courses for Undergraduates: Exemplars of Pedagogical Practices," *International Journal of Christianity & Education* 27, no. 3 (2023): 319–33.

2. Victor Norman, "Virtues and Computing," course materials for de Vries Institute Reflecting Faith course "Faith and Pedagogy," https://reflecting.faith/course/faith-and-pedagogy/. See also Klanderman et al., "Faith Integration in STEM Courses for Undergraduates"; Victor Norman, "How Will You Practice Virtue without Skill? Preparing Students to Be Virtuous Computer Programmers," *Journal of the Association of Christians in the Mathematical Sciences* (2015), https://acmsonline.org/home2/wp-content/uploads/2016/05/Teaching-Virtues-while-teaching-programming.pdf.

3. Norman, "Virtues and Computing."

4. Norman, "Virtues and Computing."

5. Norman, "Virtues and Computing."

6. Etienne Wenger, *Communities of Practice: Learning, Meaning, and Identity* (Cambridge: Cambridge University Press, 1999), 176.

7. Wenger, *Communities of Practice*, 56, 238.

8. Paul H. Thibodeau and Lera Boroditsky, "Metaphors We Think With: The Role of Metaphor in Reasoning," *PLOS ONE* 6 no. 2 (2011): e16782, https://doi.org/10.1371/journal.pone.0016782.

9. Norman, "Virtues and Computing."

10. Victor T. Norman, "Beauty and Computer Programming," *Inroads* 3 no. 1 (2012): 46–48, https://dl.acm.org/doi/abs/10.1145/2077808.2077824.

11. Klanderman et al., "Faith Integration in STEM Courses for Undergraduates"; James M. Turner, "Thinking Beautifully about Mathematics," in *Proceedings of the Association of Christians in the Mathematical Sciences 22nd Biennial Conference* (Marion, IN, 2019), 171–87; James M. Turner, "Seeing Beauty in Mathematics: On Bonaventure's 'Reduction' of Mathematics to Theology," *Cithara: Essays in the Judeo-Christian Tradition* 57, no. 1 (2017): 38–57.

12. *Didactica Magna* 33.21, my translation from Comenius, *Opera Didactica Omnia*, 1:196.

13. John Goldingay, *Psalms*, vol. 3, *Psalms 90–150* (Grand Rapids: Baker Academic, 2008), 34.

14. *Didactica Magna* 4.6, in Comenius, *Opera Didactica Omnia*, 1:20. See the notes for chapter 1 of the "Invitation" earlier in this book.

FRAMING: Implicit Stories

1. Quotations in English are from the English-Latin edition, Comenius, *Visible World*. Various later editions can be viewed digitally online, e.g., here: https://archive.org/details/orbispictusofjohoocome/page/n3/mode/2up/.

2. Comenius, *Visible World*, 5 (chapter 2).

3. Comenius, *Visible World*, 55 (chapter 44). The heading refers to these as "deformed and monstrous people."

4. Greenwood, *The London Vocabulary*, 51–63 (chapters 15–18).

5. Greenwood, *The London Vocabulary*, 123 (chapter 33).

6. Greenwood, *The London Vocabulary*, 50 (chapter 14). Unlike the chapter on the soul in the *Orbis Pictus*, this chapter has no accompanying image.

7. Taylor, *A Secular Age*.

8. Tracy D. Terrell, Erwin Tschirner, and Brigitte Nikolai, *Kontakte: A Communicative Approach, Instructor's Edition*, 5th ed. (New York: McGraw Hill, 2004).

9. Terrell, Tschirner, and Nikolai, *Kontakte*, 49, 79. The instructor's notes inform us that the focus of the second chapter is "the sts.' immediate environment outside the class," which is said to consist of "things they have, things they would like to have, and what they like to do" (79), a summary that suggests a startlingly materialistic and egocentric understanding of students' environment.

10. Terrell, Tschirner, and Nikolai, *Kontakte*, 108–69.

11. Terrell, Tschirner, and Nikolai, *Kontakte*, 268.

12. Terrell, Tschirner, and Nikolai, *Kontakte*, 404.

13. The vocabulary reference section at the back of the book includes the adjective "brave" and the verbs "to love," "to believe," and "to hope"; this is the extent of vocabulary or thematic treatment related to the cardinal or theological virtues, and even these words lack any visible virtues frame.

14. The glossary includes vocabulary for "lovable," "to be in love," "to fall in love," "lover," and "lovesickness."

15. Cf. Jennifer A. Sandlin and Peter McLaren, eds., *Critical Pedagogies of Consumption: Living and Learning in the Shadow of the "Shopocalypse"* (New York: Routledge, 2010).

FRAMING: Showing and Hiding

1. See, e.g., Jonathan Wilson, *God's Good World: Reclaiming the Doctrine of Creation* (Grand Rapids: Baker Academic, 2013), xii.

2. The images in this chapter are from Comenius, *Orbis Sensualium Pictus*, and were retrieved from Wikimedia Commons (https://commons.wikimedia.org/w/index.php?search=orbis+pictus&title=Special:MediaSearch&go=Go&type=image).

3. David I. Smith, "A Test of Character and an Enticement to Love: Comenius on Educating for Human Responsibility toward Other Creatures," in *Environmental Education: An Interdisciplinary Approach to Nature*, ed. Matthew Etherington (Eugene, OR: Wipf & Stock, 2023), 28–40.

4. Comenius, *Pampaedia*, 2.13, my translation, from John Amos Co-

menius, *De Rerum Humanorum Emendatione Consultatio Catholica* (Prague: Academia Scientiarum Bohemoslovenica, 1966).

5. Greenwood, *The London Vocabulary*, 24.

6. In the *Orbis Pictus* this is dealt with separately in a later chapter in connection with food.

7. Greenwood, *The London Vocabulary*, iii.

8. Comenius, *Visible World*, 118.

9. Greenwood, *The London Vocabulary*, 51.

10. Comenius, *Visible World*, 294.

11. Greenwood, *The London Vocabulary*, 85.

12. Kenneth V. Rosenberg et al., "Decline of the North American Avifauna," *Science* 366, no. 6461 (2019): 120–24.

ASSIGNING: Looking for Answers

1. David I. Smith et al., *Digital Life Together: The Challenge of Technology for Christian Schools* (Grand Rapids: Eerdmans, 2020), 235.

2. Jeffrey A. Roberts and David M. Wasieleski, "Moral Reasoning in Computer-Based Task Environments: Exploring the Interplay between Cognitive and Technological Factors on Individuals' Propensity to Break Rules," *Journal of Business Ethics* 110, no. 3 (2012): 355–76.

3. Francesca Gino and Bradley R. Staats, "Your Desire to Get Things Done Can Undermine Your Effectiveness," *Harvard Business Review*, March 22, 2016, https://hbr.org/2016/03/your-desire-to-get-things-done-can-undermine-your-effectiveness.

4. See, e.g., Alfie Kohn, "The Case against Grades," *Educational Leadership* 69, no. 3 (2011): 28–33.

5. Hannah Walter, EDUC 249 student journal, quoted with permission.

ASSIGNING: Here's Your Assignment

1. Paul Griffiths, *Religious Reading: The Place of Reading in the Practice of Religion* (New York: Oxford University Press, 1999); "Reading as a Spiritual Practice," in *The Scope of Our Art: The Vocation of the Theological Teacher*, ed. L. Gregory Jones and Stephanie Paulsell (Grand Rapids: Eerdmans, 2002), 32–47.

2. See Paul J. Griffiths, *The Vice of Curiosity: An Essay on Intellectual Appetite* (Winnipeg: Canadian Mennonite University Press, 2006).

3. For a useful recent discussion of the practices that we build around reading in educational contexts and how they relate to our formation, see Griffis, Ooms, and Roberts, *Deep Reading: Practices to Subvert the Vices of Our Distracted, Hostile, and Consumeristic Age*.

4. Mark Schwehn, "Liberal Learning and Christian Practical Wisdom," in *Christian Faith and University Life: Stewards of the Academy*, ed. T. Laine Scales and Jennifer L. Howell (Cham, Switzerland: Palgrave Macmillan, 2018): 73–89, here 83.

5. Schwehn, "Liberal Learning," 84.

6. Schwehn, "Liberal Learning," 84.

7. See Cynthia G. Slagter, "Approaching Interpretive Virtues through Reading Aloud," *Journal of Education and Christian Belief* 11, no. 2 (2007): 95–107, https://doi.org/10.1177/205699710701100208.

8. Mark A. Pike, "From Personal to Social Transaction: A Model of Aesthetic Reading in the Classroom," *Journal of Aesthetic Education* 37, no. 2 (2003): 61–72.

9. See https://teachfastly.com/activity-map/wonder-and-wisdom/?section=discover&activity=3.

10. See https://civichospitality.com/.

11. David I. Smith, *On Christian Teaching*, 105–6.

12. See Wolterstorff, "Peculiar Hope of the Educator," 119–30.

ASSIGNING: Teachers and Burdens

1. See David I. Smith, "Reading Practices and Christian Pedagogy: Enacting Charity with Texts," in David I. Smith and James K. A. Smith, *Teaching and Christian Practices*, 43–60.

2. Richard T. France, *The Gospel according to Matthew: An Introduction and Commentary* (Grand Rapids: Eerdmans, 1985), 324.

3. For more examples, see David I. Smith et al., "Which Student Struggles Do We Help to Create?"

PAUSING: Small Pauses

1. Doug Blomberg, "The Practice of Wisdom: Knowing When," *Journal of Education and Christian Belief* 2, no. 1 (1998): 7–26, here 9.

2. This chapter overlaps with material prepared for David I. Smith, "Just in Time: Some Reflections on Wait Time and 'Knowing When,'" in *"A Tree of Life to Those Who Embrace Her": Reflections on the Pursuit of Wisdom and the Promise of Education in Honour of Doug Blomberg*, ed. Agnes A. Struik and Nicholas Ansell (Eugene, OR: Wipf & Stock, in press).

3. Mary Budd Rowe, "Wait-Time and Rewards as Instructional Variables, Their Influence on Language, Logic, and Fate Control: Part One—Wait-Time," *Journal of Research in Science Teaching* 11, no. 2 (1974): 81–94.

4. Rowe, "Wait-Time and Rewards as Instructional Variables"; "Reflections on Wait-Time: Some Methodological Questions," *Journal of Research in Science Teaching* 11, no. 3 (1974): 263–79; "Relation of Wait-Time and Rewards to the Development of Language, Logic, and Fate Control: Part II: Rewards," *Journal of Research in Science Teaching* 11, no. 4 (1974): 291–308; "Wait Time: Slowing Down May Be a Way of Speeding Up!," *Journal of Teacher Education* 37 (1986): 43–50; "Science, Silence, and Sanctions," *Science and Children* 34, no. 1 (September 1996): 35–37.

5. Rowe, "Wait Time," 43.

6. Rowe, "Wait Time," 48.

7. Wait time has proven susceptible to being taken up as a component in templates for controlling student behavior (e.g., Robert P. Trussell, "Classroom Universals to Prevent Problem Behaviors," *Intervention in School and Clinic* 43, no. 3 [2008]: 179–85). This is in some tension with Rowe's original conception.

8. Rowe, "Wait Time," 45.

9. In *On Christian Teaching*, 120, I discussed an example of an instructor with minimal wait time failing to get discussion off the ground and falsely ascribing the classroom failure to students' tiredness or unwillingness to engage. The instructor was, I think, unconsciously engaging in a form of false witness. The instructor's story about student failure was, as far as I could ascertain, unjust. It unfairly represented the causes of the classroom dynamics, it implied unfair criticism of the students, and it deflected responsibility from the teacher's own structuring of time to the surmised vices of the young.

10. Murial Saville-Troike, "Cultural Maintenance and 'Vanishing' Languages," in *Text and Context: Cross-Disciplinary Perspectives on Language Study*, ed. Claire Kramsch and Sally McConnell-Ginet (Lexington, MA: Heath, 1992), 148–55.

11. See David I. Smith, *On Christian Teaching*, 114.

PAUSING: Pausing for Breath

1. David I. Smith et al., *Digital Life Together*.

2. David I. Smith et al., *Digital Life Together*, 119–36.

3. For a different example of intentional pauses for thought, see Peter Alonzi, "Pauses," in *Becoming Beholders: Cultivating Sacramental Imagination and Actions in College Classrooms*, ed. Karen E. Eifler and Thomas M. Landy (Collegeville, MN: Liturgical Press, 2014), 86–99.

4. Terry L. Erwin and Janice C. Scott, "Seasonal and Size Patterns, Trophic Structure, and Richness of Coleoptera in the Tropical Arboreal Ecosystem: The Fauna of the Tree Luehea seemannii Triana and Planch in the Canal Zone of Panama," *Coleopterists Bulletin* 34, no. 3 (1980): 305–22.

PAUSING: Pausing for Connection

1. John Wesley, *Letter to a Friend, Concerning Tea* (London: A. MacIntosh, 1825).

2. If memory serves, I think I learned this practice from Dorothy Vaandering.

3. Jane Kelly Rodeheffer, "'Expound This Love': Forming the Next Generation of Christian Teacher-Scholars through the Lilly Graduate Fellows Program," in *Called to Teach: Excellence, Commitment, and Community in Christian Higher Education*, ed. Christopher J. Richmann and J. Lenore Wright (Eugene, OR: Pickwick, 2020), 131–48, here 143.

4. Cheryl Glenn, *Unspoken: A Rhetoric of Silence* (Carbondale: Southern Illinois University Press, 2004).

5. On vainglory, see Rebecca Konyndyk DeYoung, *Vainglory: The Forgotten Vice* (Grand Rapids: Eerdmans, 2014).

6. Rebecca Konyndyk DeYoung, "Pedagogical Rhythms: Practices and Reflections on Practice," in David I. Smith and James K. A. Smith, *Teaching and Christian Practices*, 24–42, here 32–33.

7. DeYoung, "Pedagogical Rhythms," 33.

8. David I. Smith et al., *Digital Life Together*, 240.

9. David I. Smith et al., *Digital Life Together*, 241.

10. Paige Bokach, comment on course discussion board, IDIS 170-14, 2020, quoted with permission.

11. Pamela Tumwebaze, video interview for course materials for the de

Vries Institute Reflecting Faith course "Faith and Online Pedagogy," 2022, https://reflecting.faith/course/faith-and-online-pedagogy/.

PAUSING: Pausing for Hospitality

1. The material in this chapter has also appeared in David I. Smith and Joyce Azaki, "Hospitality, Teaching, and Pauses for Reflection," *Christ Animating Learning Blog*, March 25, 2024, https://christianscholars.com/hospitality-teaching-and-pauses-for-reflection/.

REPEATING: Rhythms of Imagination

1. Elizabeth Conde-Frazier, *Atando Cabos: Latinx Contributions to Theological Education* (Grand Rapids: Eerdmans, 2021).

2. Conde-Frazier, *Atando Cabos*, 2.

3. Conde-Frazier, *Atando Cabos*, 3.

4. Conde-Frazier, *Atando Cabos*, 4.

5. N. T. Wright, *Colossians and Philemon*, Tyndale NT Commentaries (Leicester, UK: Inter-Varsity Press, 1987), 79–80.

6. James Gilchrist Lawson, *Deeper Experiences of Famous Christians* (Anderson, IN: Warner, 1911); George Maunder, *Eminent Christian Philanthropists: Brief Biographical Sketches Designed Especially as Studies for the Young* (London: Wesleyan Conference Office, n.d.) (published before 1878).

REPEATING: Rhythms of Seeing

1. Joanna Ziegler, "Practice Makes Reception: The Role of Contemplative Ritual in Approaching Art," in Eifler and Landy, *Becoming Beholders*, 41–55.

2. Cited in Ziegler, "Practice Makes Reception," 42.

3. Kevin Gary argues that if we are to be drawn out of the boredom arising from consumerist despair, we need to be apprenticed to structures and disciplines that draw us into perceiving differently, and for this to happen we need to be held accountable by a wise partner. See Kevin Hood Gary, *Why Boredom Matters: Education, Leisure, and the Quest for a Meaningful Life* (Cambridge: Cambridge University Press, 2022), 96–97.

4. Ziegler, "Practice Makes Reception," 52.

5. Ziegler, "Practice Makes Reception," 51.

6. This does not go as far as Simone Weil's famous argument that "prayer consists of attention," that disciplined attention is a form of self-emptying, and that the kind of disciplined attention that a student can develop through learning is itself a kind of preparation for prayer. Simone Weil, "Reflections on the Right Use of School Studies with a View to the Love of God," in *Waiting for God* (New York: Harper Perennial Modern Classics, 2009), 105–16. For a usefully different account with important contrasts, see Alan Jacobs, "Bakhtin and the Hermeneutics of Love," in *Bakhtin and Religion: A Feeling for Faith*, ed. Susan M. Felch and Paul J. Contino (Evanston, IL: Northwestern University Press, 2001), 25–45.

7. David I. Smith et al., *Digital Life Together*, 98.

8. Missy Bryan, personal communication, quoted with permission.

REPEATING: Rhythms of Reading

1. There has recently been a small surge in books about reading as a practice worth investing ourselves in for the sake of our formation. See, for example, Karen Swallow Prior, *On Reading Well: Finding the Good Life through Great Books* (Grand Rapids: Brazos, 2018); Jessica Hooten Wilson, *Reading for the Love of God* (Grand Rapids: Brazos, 2023); Griffis, Ooms, and Roberts, *Deep Reading*.

2. For broader discussion of the ideas here, see David I. Smith, "Reading Practices and Christian Pedagogy: Enacting Charity with Texts," in David I. Smith and James K. A. Smith, *Teaching and Christian Practices*, 43–60.

3. See ASSIGNING.

4. Wenger, *Communities of Practice*, 56.

5. Mikhail M. Bakhtin, *Toward a Philosophy of the Act*, trans. Vadim Liapunov (Austin: University of Texas Press, 1993), 64. On Bakhtin's relationship to Christianity, see Ruth Coates, *Christianity in Bakhtin: God and the Exiled Author* (Cambridge: Cambridge University Press, 1998); Alexandar Mihailovic, *Corporeal Words: Mikhail Bakhtin's Theology of Discourse* (Evanston, IL: Northwestern University Press, 1997).

ENDING: Thinking Backward

1. Bertolt Brecht, *Stories of Mr. Keuner*, trans. Martin Chalmers (San Francisco: City Lights Books, 2001), 16.

2. Brecht, *Stories of Mr. Keuner*, 16.

3. For an example from a science classroom designed by my colleague Crystal Bruxvoort, see "Delve Activities," Fastly, accessed May 9, 2024, https://teachfastly.com/activity-map/models-humility-and-truth/?section=delve&activity=3.

4. Charles Taylor, *Modern Social Imaginaries* (Durham, NC: Duke University Press, 2004).

ENDING: Seeking Congruence

1. See John Shortt, "The Rationale of the Charis Project," in *Spiritual and Religious Education*, ed. Mal Leicester, Celia Modgill, and Sohan Modgill (London: Falmer, 2000), 160–70.

2. This unit appears in David Baker et al., *Charis Deutsch: Einheiten 1–5* (St. Albans, UK: ACT, 1996).

3. For a decade now my teaching has been in education rather than language classes, though I still train language teachers and provide demonstrations for them.

4. The following narrative is adapted from the account in David I. Smith et al., "Of Log Cabins, Fallen Bishops, and Tenacious Parents: (Auto)biographical Narrative and the Spirituality of Language Learning," in *Spirituality, Social Justice, and Language Learning*, ed. David I. Smith and Terry A. Osborn (Greenwich, CT: Information Age Publishing, 2007), 107–29. This example is also discussed in Glanzer and Alleman, *The Outrageous Idea of Christian Teaching*, 93.

5. Baker et al., *Charis Deutsch*, 59.

ENDING: Judging and Blessing

1. See Paul Griffiths, "From Curiosity to Studiousness: Catechizing the Appetite for Learning," in David I. Smith and James K. A. Smith, *Teaching and Christian Practices*, 102–22; Paul Gutacker et al., "A Symposium on Teaching Virtue: Interdisciplinary Perspectives on Pedagogy, Liturgy, and Moral Formation," *International Journal of Christianity & Education* 23, no. 2 (2019): 204–30; James K. A. Smith, *Desiring the Kingdom: Worship, Worldview, and Cultural Formation* (Grand Rapids: Baker Academic, 2009).

2. Schultze, *Servant Teaching*, 21.

3. Abraham Joshua Heschel, *The Sabbath: Its Meaning for Modern Man* (New York: Farrar, Straus & Co., 1951), 8. I discuss Heschel's image with further examples in David I. Smith, *On Christian Teaching*, 114–27.

CLOSE: Learn to Be Wise

1. Comenius, *Visible World*, 194.
2. Cf. Andrew Piper, *Book Was There: Reading in Electronic Times* (Chicago: University of Chicago Press, 2012).

INDEX